Scaffolding Young Writers

Scaffolding Young Writers

A Writers' Workshop Approach

Linda J. Dorn • Carla Soffos

Stenhouse Publishers
Portland, Maine

Stenhouse Publishers
www.stenhouse.com

Library of Congress Cataloging-in-Publication Data
Dorn, Linda J.
   Scaffolding Young Writers : a writers' work-
   shop approach / Linda J. Dorn, Carla Soffos.
      p. cm.
   Includes bibliographical references and index.
   ISBN 1-57110-342-2 (alk. paper)
   1. English language—Composition and exercises
   —Study and teaching (Primary) I. Soffos, Carla.
   II. Title.
   LB1528.D67 2001
   372.62'3044—dc21   2001042983

Cover design by Richard Hannus, Hannus Design
Associates
Cover photographs by Carla Soffos
Figure 3.4 by Matthew Uyeda

Manufactured in the United States of America on
acid-free paper

14 13 12 11 10 09 08 07   16 15 14 13 12 11 10

This book is dedicated to the many Arkansas teachers who have shared their knowledge and experience with us.

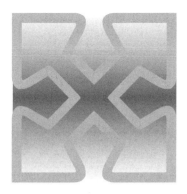

Contents

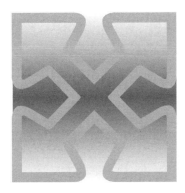

Acknowledgments

In writing this book, we recognize the work of other educators who have influenced our professional lives. First, we acknowledge the teachings of Donald Graves, Lucy Calkins, and Ralph Fletcher—from them, we have acquired knowledge of the writing process and tools for implementing writers' workshop in our classrooms. Also, we acknowledge the tremendous influence of Lev Vygotsky (1978)—through his work, we've learned the importance of language in promoting literacy, the need to work in children's learning zones, and the role of instruction in developing self-regulated learners. His theories permeate our work, specifically as they relate to the cognitive and social aspects of teaching and learning. Most important, we acknowledge the enormous influence of Marie Clay on our teaching—through her work, we've learned the importance of building on the strengths of young learners. Marie has taught us to look for changes over time in the development of a literacy system, and she has cautioned us to hold a tentative theory, one that can be continually tested with observations of children in the process of learning. Through Marie Clay's work, we have learned

the importance of teaching for strategy development, continual and ongoing assessment to guide instruction, and focusing on processing versus items of learning.

These acknowledgments would not be complete without recognizing a special group of teachers who have worked alongside us in the Arkansas Literacy Coaching Model. We would like to express our sincere thanks to the first group of Arkansas literacy coaches. These talented teachers have enthusiastically shared their knowledge and classroom experiences with us. On a moment's notice, they have sent us writing samples and videotaped examples of mini-lessons and writing conferences. As we wrote this book, the literacy coaches were there for us, only a phone call or an e-mail away. Their numerous trips to Little Rock and the daily listserv discussions are a testament to the hard work and commitment of these teachers. During the past two years, this group has held a tentative theory, one that was revisited and refined as we problem-solved together on teaching and learning issues. We thank you— Kim Mitchell, Laura McKinney, Donnie Skinner, Sue Tilley, Annita Bogard, and Angela Owen—

for your dedication and belief in children and teachers. Together, these talented educators are creating real change in Arkansas schools.

Also, we offer our heartfelt thanks to Stephanie Copes and Mike Moss, the literacy coaches at the University of Arkansas at Little Rock. Without these two committed educators, our work in schools would be incomplete. Thank you, Stephanie, for your problem-solving attitude and your enthusiasm for the writing process. Mike, thank you for your willingness to learn about new areas of technology and research. Additionally, we offer a special thanks to Debbie Williams, our university colleague, who has worked alongside us in implementing the literacy coaching model. Thank you, Debbie, for your willingness to manage this project as well as for your knowledge in literacy. Also, we acknowledge Teresa Treat, our friend and a first-grade teacher at Jim Stone Elementary, for sharing her classroom experiences and students' work with us. Teresa is a lifelong learner and a masterful teacher. Thank you, Teresa, for your continued support of our literacy initiative. A final acknowledgment goes to Krista Underwood, our friend and colleague at the Arkansas Department of Education. Krista's belief in children and teachers is evident in her words and actions. These dedicated and passionate educators are making a difference in the literacy lives of Arkansas children and teachers.

As always, we acknowledge the help of the Stenhouse team. During the process of writing this book, we've been mentored in *how* to teach writers' workshop to our students. Our personal experiences with writing have carried over to classroom teaching of children. To Philippa Stratton, our editor, and Martha Drury, our production manager, you've taught us some valuable lessons about publishing that we've incorporated into our work with young writers; for example, the student publishing checklist was revised to include text layout and paragraph organization. We thought about how you supported us in writing; and we applied the same understandings to the teaching of young writers. For instance, as we revised our lead paragraphs, our mini-lessons with students shifted to include these experiences. Through writing, we've learned more about the writing process, and we're becoming better teachers of writing to our youngest students. So, again, thank you, Philippa and Martha, for scaffolding us in the writing process. And to the entire staff at Stenhouse, thank you for your support of our work, with special thanks to Tom Seavey, our marketing director, who has worked diligently to spread our theories and practices to teachers across the country.

Finally, we thank our families for scaffolding us as we spent many long hours on writing two books. Without your encouragement and patience, we could not have accomplished this.

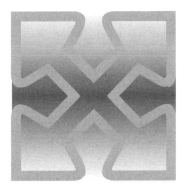

Introduction

What makes this book on writers' workshop different? We have been teachers of writing for most of our educational careers, and we've read many books on the writing process. Although we've experienced success with most of our students, we've not always been as successful with our lowest-performing writers. Too often, we've observed struggling writers become passive writers, simply because they did not have the necessary strategies, knowledge, and skills to help themselves. As we've learned more about how children learn, we've incorporated these lessons into our teaching of writing. We've tried to present a practical book that is grounded in sociocognitive learning theories. Here are some major themes throughout this book.

- The act of writing is a cognitive process that involves comprehension of ideas, expressive language, and mechanical skills.
- All writing instruction must be based on what children already know. Anything less can promote passive learners who feel inadequate about writing.

- Teachers must provide young writers with assisted and unassisted opportunities to learn about writing. First, the child accomplishes a task with teacher assistance; then the child accomplishes the task alone. The writing environment is structured to allow for the transfer of knowledge, skills, and strategies from assisted to unassisted learning zones.

In Chapter 1, we discuss how children become writers and the tension that can occur between early transcribing and composing processes. We present benchmark behaviors that children exhibit as they become more competent at orchestrating the writing process. The goal of writing instruction is to create conditions that promote self-regulated writers who understand how to guide and monitor their own writing. Writing instruction that includes explicit language in how to use relevant resources can provide young writers with self-help tools for regulating their own work.

In Chapter 2, we describe the link between assessment and instruction. Teachers must know how to observe writing behavior for changes over time. They can use assessment to find out what children know, plan instruction based on their strengths and needs, and evaluate how well teaching has influenced students' learning. Teachers should understand that changes in writing behavior can represent changes in a student's understanding of the writing process. In this chapter we present teachers with formal and informal writing assessments, including writing rubrics and checklists from kindergarten through third grade. Also we share examples of students' work in the three modes of writing: expressive, transactional, and poetic.

Chapter 3 provides teachers with a road map for implementing writers' workshop in the primary grades. We discuss ways to organize and manage a writers' workshop, including how to introduce a writers' notebook and writing forms. Routines and procedures for daily writing are established and students expect writing to be a regular part of their lives.

Chapter 4 focuses on the role of mini-lessons for shaping writing development. Young writers need explicit teaching with clear and relevant demonstrations. Too many new things to learn can overload the child's working memory and interfere with sustained learning. Instruction should be aimed at the writer's zone of proximal development (Vygotsky 1978). In this chapter, we present four categories of mini-lessons: organization, strategies, skills, and author's craft.

Chapter 5 emphasizes the importance of talking with children about their writing. During writing conferences, teachers provide support that is aimed at a student's zone of proximal development. If a writer does not understand the intention of instruction, the teacher must scaffold the student in ways that allow him to develop some degree of understanding. The level of teacher scaffolding is adjusted according to the needs of the young writer. The writing conference plays a critical role in developing self-regulated writers.

All the ideas and theories in this text have been applied by teachers in primary classrooms. Our purpose in writing this book has been to provide teachers with some details and valuable resources for implementing a successful writers' workshop.

The Development of Young Writers

When Jessica, my [Linda's] granddaughter, was three years old, she kept a journal with markers and crayons on the bottom shelf of the bookcase in my office. Very quickly, she learned that the journal was a place where she could record messages; and she knew that the scribbles on the page represented something very important. As I worked in my office, she worked alongside me, writing notes, letters, stories. On her fifth birthday, I was presenting at a conference, so we had planned to have her birthday party on the following weekend. On Friday, I received a telephone call from Jessica, who informed me that she was mad because I had missed her birthday. Again, I told her how sad I was, but on Saturday we would have her birthday party. Saturday came; she was happy with her presents; but later that afternoon, she decided to write me a letter—a reminder that I had missed her birthday. She went into my office, got her journal and markers, then informed me, "Nana, I'm writing you a letter. 'Cause you forgot my birthday." "What are you going to say in your letter?" I asked. She responded, "I'm mad at you 'cause you forgot my birthday." After she finished her letter, I

inquired, "Can I read it now?" "No," she answered, "'cause I need something to put it in." "An envelope?" I asked. "Yes," she said, "I need an envelope." My husband, Jan, handed her an envelope, and she crumpled the letter into uneven folds and shoved it into the envelope. Again, I asked, "Can I read my letter now?" In a firm tone, she explained, "I have to put your name on it." Then she asked, "How do you write *Nana*?" I said, "Just write it the way you think it would look." She accepted my response, addressed the envelope, and handed it to me: "Now you can read it. And that's so you won't ever forget my birthday again!"

What does Jessica know about writing? First, she knows that writing is a meaningful and functional task. When she has something to say, she can write her words down for someone to read. She understands the power and permanence of putting her thoughts on paper, and she knows that a letter is one way she can communicate her message. Also, she knows that she can address the letter to a specific person. She understands the purpose of writing even before she has acquired the mechanical skills to transcribe her message in conventional forms. At barely five years old, Jessica is a writer.

The Social and Cognitive Sides of Writing

Writing is by nature a social process. Writing represents the means by which a message can be communicated to someone else. Children learn how to become writers through meaningful interactions with more knowledgeable people. In an environment where writing is an everyday occurrence, young children learn important lessons about the writing process. They begin to talk about their transcriptions as signs of meaning. They make inquiries such as, "What does this say?" or "How do you make my name?" These early observations about print are the foundations for learning how to write. If children come from a writing environment prior to first grade, they have already acquired critical understandings for learning about the writing process.

In her book for parents, Healy (1994) describes the cognitive side of the writing process. First, she explains, the child must understand and pull together ideas or knowledge. This implies that the child must search his own memories for the information he desires to communicate. These ideas can be global representations of feelings, emotions, and images. Language becomes a tool for consolidating bigger ideas into original statements while choosing the best words and placing them in the correct order. This complex process is driven by a personal need to express a "just right" message. For the beginning writer, Healy explains how the child must hold the ideas in working memory long enough to transcribe the message. This becomes a challenge if the child has limited transcribing skills. Yet, if the message is

meaningful and personal, the child is less likely to forget it while dealing with the mechanical aspects of recording. The child's ability to orchestrate the social, cognitive, and mechanical sides of writing are mediated by a more knowledgeable person, who scaffolds the child at appropriate points in the writing process.

Writing is a learned skill that is shaped through practice and constructive feedback. It requires motivation, strategies, skills, and knowledge. When children write, they acquire cognitive strategies for attending, monitoring, searching, evaluating, and self-correcting their actions (Clay 2001). A self-regulated writer is one who knows how to guide and monitor her writing actions toward achieving a specific writing goal. This implies that the self-regulated writer understands how to use specific strategies for planning, generating, organizing, and revising the writing process (Harris and Graham 1999).

The Writing Process

In teaching writing to young children, we must recognize the complexity of the process. Think a moment about what happens in the mind of a writer as he creates a written piece. The intricacy becomes clear when we apply this concept to our own writing. The first step, that of coming up with the idea, is based on our experiences and knowledge—in other words, our thoughts. These ideas can be spontaneous, elaborated, or general. In either case, the next step, that of finding the right words to express the idea, is a more challenging task. This involves rereading and revising the text, for example, deleting unnecessary words or sections, rearranging sentences and paragraphs, and clarifying concepts. Here, the writer must always consider the needs and experiences of the reader: this drives the purpose of the writing act. Throughout the process, a writer applies strategies of organizing, monitoring, and revising with a goal of communicating a specific message to a particular audience. This is a learned process, a skill that develops over time and requires good models, extensive practice, and constructive feedback from others.

For the beginning writer, the difficult part is finding the right words and phrases to express the ideas in logical and sequential ways while simultaneously dealing with the mechanical limitations of transcribing the message. The tension that can occur between the mechanics of recording and composing the message can affect how children (and teachers) view the writing process (Smith 1994). For instance, from a mechanical perspective, a young child's writing might look accurate, but the composition could lack depth or variety. As teachers, we can all relate to the child who writes the same story day after day using the same known words. For these children, neat handwriting and accurate spellings represent their theory of writing. On the other hand, for the child who focuses exclusively on the message but lacks the skills for transcribing the words, the message can be impossible to read. The challenge for the teacher is to validate the composition while teaching for the transcription of the mechanical skills. Here, the goal of writing is to develop a well-orchestrated process that depends on the interrelatedness of three aspects of writing (Healy 1994):

- Comprehension of ideas
- Expressive language
- Facility with mechanics

Let's apply this theory to two beginning writers. In the first example (Figure 1.1), Heather, a first-grade student, has composed a story about losing her Beanie Babies at day care. The narrative reflects a personal experi-

Figure 1.1 Heather's writing sample (first grade).

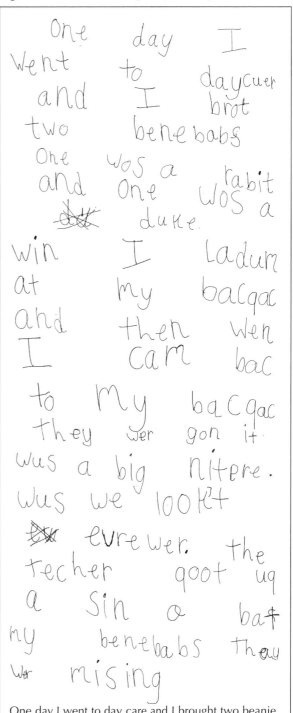

One day I went to day care and I brought two beanie babies. One was a rabbit and one was a duck. When I laid them at my backpack and then when I came back to my backpack, they were gone. It was a big nightmare. Once we looked everywhere. The teacher put up a sign about my beanie babies. They were missing.

ence, one that is meaningful and relevant to her. As a result, Heather uses vocabulary and sentence structures that are consistent with her oral language. She develops her topic with fluency and ease; furthermore, she sustains the idea (losing her Beanie Babies) throughout the piece. She uses time cues and complex sentence structures to create a transitional flow (*one day, once we looked, and then*). Her piece contains about sixty words, including seventeen different high-frequency words that are spelled correctly. Moreover, Heather shows an ability to apply strategies for solving unknown words, including compound words, multisyllabic words, digraphs, and blended sounds. We can assume from Heather's piece that her theory of writing is a message-making theory. In the process of composing a meaningful message, Heather is acquiring knowledge for transcribing her ideas in more conventional language. During conferences with her teacher, Heather will sharpen her mechanical skills as a writer; at the same time, she will refine her ability to compose more sophisticated texts.

Now let's compare Heather's writing to that of another first-grade writer (Figure 1.2). What is this child's theory of writing? Since the goal of writing is to communicate images and ideas, does this piece meet the writing goal? In contrast to Heather's message, this particular composition lacks depth and emotion. Also, if we compare the structure and vocabulary, we can see a dramatic difference, for this piece consists of four sentences that are similar in structure and word choices. The entire piece contains only sixteen words, nine of them different. All words are familiar, one-syllable words; therefore, this text does not provide the young writer with opportunities to try out strategies for unknown spellings. From this sample, we can assume that the child's theory of writing is one of neat handwriting and accurate spellings.

Figure 1.2 A first-grade writing sample.

When teaching writing to young children, teachers must strive to create a balance between composing and transcribing skills. If our teaching becomes unbalanced, this will influence how children view the writing process. The ultimate goal of teaching is to promote an orchestration process. It is important to note that orchestration occurs at the point where old knowledge meets new knowledge: if the child has too many new things to learn, this can interfere with the orchestration process. The primary grades are critical times for shaping orchestration. When teachers analyze children's writing, they can design their writing program based on what children already know and what they need to know to move their writing forward.

Table 1.1 lists the cognitive and perceptual challenges that young writers must deal with as they attempt to orchestrate the writing process. These phases are not intended to be static, for the process is much too complex to place in a sequence. However, in our experiences with young writers, we have found that children exhibit specific benchmark behaviors along a continuum of writing control. The processes of composing, transcribing, editing, and revising work together to shape writing knowledge. This implies that teachers must recognize behaviors that indicate how students are becoming writers; and we must teach for the orchestration of the writing processes (see

Table 1.1 Orchestrating the Writing Process in Narrative Writing

Composing (Writing Fluency)	Transcribing (Encoding)	Editing and Revising
Emergent Writers	**Emergent Writers**	**Emergent Writers**
Generates topic or idea with teacher assistance	Attends to early concepts about print	Edits by crossing out letters or partially known words (e.g., name, high-frequency word)
Uses an emerging sense of writer's voice based on oral language structures	Attends to letter formation	Edits by trying out letters and experiments with recording new words
Holds the language in memory while transcribing the message	Says words slowly	
Returns to the beginning of the sentence; rereads to remember the next word	Hears and records sounds in words (not necessarily in sequential order)	
Writes a simple message of one to three sentences	Uses resources to help with transcribing letters and words (e.g., ABC chart, name chart, word book)	
Beginning Early Writers	**Beginning Early Writers**	**Beginning Early Writers**
Generates topics or ideas with or without teacher assistance	Records letters and known words more fluently	Edits by crossing out unwanted letters and words
Begins to use a topic list to record ideas	Analyzes unknown words using slow articulation	Edits by circling words that do not look right
Holds ideas in memory while transcribing the message	Records letters in word sequence	Revises message by adding a word or two to the text
Records series of events in chronological order from beginning to end (e.g., bed-to-bed)	Tries out spellings on practice page	
Uses simple transition words to support time flow	Spells most high-frequency words accurately	
Uses dialogue		
Late Early Writers	**Late Early Writers**	**Late Early Writers**
Creates an opening sentence or phrase that leads into the writing (*once upon a time, last night, one day*)	Attends to spelling patterns; records words more fluently	Edits by recording word attempts on the spelling trial page
Develops and maintains the idea throughout the piece		Edits by looking up circled words in a simple dictionary
Begins to experiment with using descriptive words, strong nouns, and muscular verbs		Uses forms in writing notebook to assist with better word choices
Begins to develop an awareness of writer's voice		Uses a writing checklist to edit and revise writing
Ends with a closing statement (*the end, that was a good day*)		Revises message by using caret ^ to add new words or ideas to the text
Begins to develop an awareness for publishing criteria		Revises message by deleting some words and using proofreading techniques, such as drawing a line through unwanted text
		Uses publishing checklist to prepare a piece for publication

Table 1.1 Orchestrating the Writing Process in Narrative Writing *(continued)*

Transitional Writers	Transitional Writers	Transitional Writers
Uses good leads that grab the attention of the reader	Attends to word meanings	Creates and revises multiple drafts of leads
Uses strong nouns and muscular verbs	Increased speed and accuracy	Revises word choices and substitutes richer vocabulary
Uses descriptive language to create mind pictures	Spells most unknown words according to word parts	Revises message by eliminating redundant and unnecessary information
Uses transitional words and phrases for time flow		Revises and groups ideas by rearranging words, sentences, or phrases; uses proofreading tools such as cut-and-paste, asterisks, circles, and lines to group ideas
Recognizes and applies writer's voice		
Ties text together with interesting or creative endings		Uses editing and revising checklists
Understands and applies publishing criteria in preparing a piece for an audience		Uses dictionaries and thesauruses
		Incorporates revisions and editing into final draft
		Increases accuracy of final draft

Dorn and Soffos 2001a). Teachers can ask four simple questions to promote this process:

>What is easy for the writer to do?
>What is hard for the writer to do?
>What does the teacher expect the writer to do?
>What does the teacher expect to do for the writer?

As an example, let's apply this concept to the task of revision. First, it is important to keep in mind that revision relates to the meaning level (in contrast to editing at the mechanical level). In scaffolding young writers, the revising process can occur along a continuum of easier to harder tasks:

- *Adding words to a text is easier to do.* Therefore, the teacher can introduce a caret and show the students how to use this mark for inserting a word or two within their text.

- *Deleting words from a text is harder to do; deleting lines or phrases is even more difficult.* That's because young writers have worked hard to record longer stories, and they think every word is important. This revision skill is more difficult because it requires writers to think critically about their piece and eliminate unnecessary words or phrases that can muddy the message. As writers develop longer texts (mostly chronological recounts rather than stories), the teacher can scaffold them to think about the main idea of the text and introduce proofreading techniques (e.g., lines drawn through phrases or words) that support the revising process.

- *Substituting words for other words is more difficult because it requires writers to know multiple meanings for words.* This complex skill is developed as teachers provide young writers with opportunities to develop rich vocabularies and explore word meanings. During mini-lessons and writing conferences, the teacher guides young writers to think about better word choices and use resources as tools for examining word meanings (see Chapter 3).

- *Rearranging sentences and paragraphs is the most difficult skill.* To accomplish this sophisticated task, writers must understand how to organize smaller details under a bigger idea, including knowledge for how sentences and paragraphs are grouped into related themes. For beginning writers, teachers can scaffold this process with mini-lessons and conferences that focus on simple cut-and-paste techniques that allow writers to physically move their text around. At the same time, teachers provide explicit lessons in proofreading techniques, such as asterisks for inserting new information and circles and lines for rearranging texts.

In this example of revision, we've illustrated the change over time that can occur as the writer becomes more skilled at organizing and communicating her ideas. For the proficient writer, the process is working smoothly, simply because the writer has developed control of the transcribing process, and she can devote her attention to the craft of writing. However, along the way to proficiency, it serves us well as teachers to consider the cognitive and mechanical demands on beginning writers as they refine their composition skills.

Levels of Writing Competence

The Emergent Writer

At the emergent level, the greatest challenge occurs with transcribing the message: writing letters and words, hearing and recording sounds in words, and conventions of print (spacing, directional movement across print).

With teacher guidance, the emergent writer learns to use simple resources (ABC charts, name charts, word books) to assist problem-solving efforts. When teachers coach emergent writers to cross out letters and experiment with new words, they are building editing skills. These risk-taking behaviors are the basis for early monitoring, searching, and self-correcting actions, all of which are the foundation for successful writing. Here, children's stories are short enough to be held in memory as they deal with the mechanical issues of getting the message on paper. Using their oral language as a scaffold for written language, children expect writing to be meaningful and functional. Therefore, they practice rereading behaviors that allow them to make logical and realistic predictions for the upcoming words and phrases. The goal—that of making meaning—is achieved as young writers work to create a balance between composing and transcribing the message. (See Figure 1.3 for a writing sample by an emergent writer.)

Figure 1.3 A writing sample by an emergent writer.

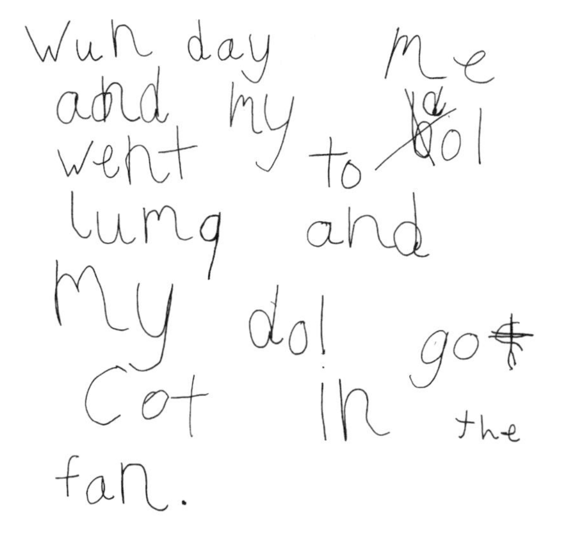

One day me and my doll went to jump and my doll got caught in the fan.

The Early Writer

As young writers acquire more skill with print, they can attend more actively to the composing process. About this time, they begin to think about the length of their stories; in many cases, they fill in the page with repetitive words and structures that resemble the patterned (stylized) stories they are reading. Here, it is common for children to evaluate their work with comments such as, "Look at how many pages I wrote!" or "I wrote a lot today!" Generally, this phase is followed by the bed-to-bed story where children's writing consists of an account of the day from the time they get up in the morning until they go to bed at night. Here is a classic example of a bed-to-bed story written by Mary Catherine, a first-grade writer:

> "What a day," I said. "It is Easter Sunday." I ran into my mom's bedroom. I jumped on her bed. I said, "Wake up." My mom woke up. I said, "It is Easter." Then we went into the living room. I saw my Easter basket. I saw my brother's basket too. It had a lot of things in it. Then my dad woke up. He said, "Happy Easter." He looked into my basket. He said, "You got a lot of toys." I said to my mom, "Can I fly my kite." My mom said, "No you can't." So I did not get to fly my kite that day. It was okay. My mom said, "Maybe another time." Then my grandmother came over to my house to eat with us. Then we got to eat strawberries. I got to eat my strawberries in my mom and my dad's bedroom. Then my grandmother went home. Then I put my bowl in the sink. Then I went back into my mom's and my dad's bedroom. I played with the bunnies. It was fun. Then my mom said, "It is time for you to get to bed." Before I went to bed my mom read a book to me. Then I went to bed.

From these chronological accounts, young writers learn how to select one event and develop the idea. When this happens, the writing becomes shorter and more focused. In the following example, written six weeks later, Mary Catherine focuses her attention on one idea (learning to ride her bike) and sustains this theme throughout her writing piece:

> One day my mom was teaching me to ride my bike without training wheels. I didn't know how to ride my bike without training wheels. I tried but I kept falling off my bike. My mom leaned over me so I would not fall off. I started to fall but my mom caught me. I rode my bike for a long way and then my mom let go of my bike. I did not fall off. I had a great day riding my bike!

The benefits of writing longer texts are evident in the increased number of words the child writes. As a result, the transcribing process becomes smoother and more automatic. Now the writer records letters and words with greater ease, analyzes unknown words using slow articulation, and records letters in word sequence. The very act of writing increases the child's attention to print; thus, the young writer begins to notice more about the visual information. This leads to early editing strategies—a time when the writer begins to circle words that do not look right. It is important to note that early writers do not have to correct all words; instead they are learning to self-monitor their work, thus laying the foundation for more overt searching and self-correcting behaviors. In writers' workshop, students learn the importance of recording ideas fluently in first drafts and then applying editing and revising techniques to refine the message.

The early writer moves along a continuum that reflects greater skill with the writing process, including good opening sentences, better word choices (descriptive words, nouns, and verbs), and a sense of closure. About the same time, the teacher introduces the early writer to new resources, including writing forms and checklists (see Chapter 3). These tools serve as self-help guides to promote independent thinking. The important point is that the child must possess the knowledge and skills to use these resources in productive ways.

The Transitional Writer

At the transitional level, the transcribing skills of young writers are faster and more automatic. This control frees their attention to focus more actively on the craft of writing. By this time, the writer has acquired greater competence with the processes of writing, including composing multiple drafts, editing and revising techniques, incorporating changes into the final version, and preparing a piece for publication. The transitional writer is able to pull out specific sections from a draft and attend more closely to specific details within the writing piece, for example, creating good leads that grab the reader's attention and developing vivid settings and characters (see Chapter 4). During revision, writers rearrange sentences and paragraphs, substitute richer vocabulary, use strong nouns, muscular verbs, and descriptive language to create mind pictures. The transitional writer has become more efficient at orchestrating the processes of writing.

Closing Thoughts

In developing independent writers, we must consider the cognitive and social sides to learning. Since all new learning is grounded in old learning experiences, teachers must be attuned to what the child already knows. Thus, the writer learns how to use existing knowledge to guide and regulate new learning activity. In the process, knowledge becomes organized into a well-orchestrated network of related experiences. The important point is that the writer can access this knowledge more efficiently and rapidly because of its interrelated nature (in contrast to isolated information). For us, as teachers, the goal of writing instruction is to provide young writers with opportunities for learning about the processes of writing.

Assessing Writing Development

The link between assessment and instruction is indissoluble because we cannot plan writing instruction for our students without understanding what they know about the writing process. Teachers should create instructional opportunities that allow students to apply problem-solving solutions to their writing. In scaffolding young writers, primary teachers must

- Recognize and understand the developmental changes that occur over time as the writer becomes more competent in a particular area
- Understand the role of the curriculum in shaping the writing development of young children

In this chapter, the assessment of writing is influenced by a process-oriented theory. If children are not progressing as writers, then we must examine our writing program for the opportunities it provides them to learn about writing. To assess children's writing development, we can ask questions, such as

Do they have a habit of writing? Do they choose to write?

Can they select their own topics?

Do they understand the writing process, including prewriting, first draft, revising, editing, final draft, and publication?

Do they know how to use editing checklists and rubrics to evaluate their own writing?

Do they use resources, such as dictionaries and thesauruses, to check their spelling and vocabulary?

Do they understand the craft of writing? Do they read like a writer?

Do they attend to the writing techniques and language used by their favorite authors?

Can they write for different purposes? Do they understand how to organize their writing to accommodate a particular audience? Can they use knowledge of text genre to plan their writing?

Do they use spelling that is developmentally appropriate for their grade level?

Is their language appropriate for their grade level?

Formal Assessments of Primary-Grade Writers

Based on these questions and standards from the New Standards Primary Committee (1999), we worked with classroom teachers and literacy coaches to develop end-of-year rubrics to assess the writing development of primary students who were in writers' workshop classrooms. During the first year, we scored 245 first-grade writing samples; during the second year, we scored over 1,500 first-grade writing samples and over 250 second-grade writing samples. In the process, we refined some of the categories, eliminated redundant categories, and placed quantitative parameters (e.g., "some" versus "all") around particular areas of competence. Our goal was to develop a standardized tool that would allow us to examine young students' understanding of the writing process.

The rubrics were categorized to cover three areas of writing development: (1) process and habits, (2) audience, purpose, and author's craft, and (3) language use and conventions (see Appendix A). Here, we use the rubrics to examine the writing processes of first-, second-, and third-grade students.

Under Standard I, primary students were assessed on their understanding of the writing process, including first draft, revising, editing, and final draft criteria. Under Standard II, students were assessed on their knowledge of the writing craft, specifically their ability to compose a focused piece of writing with a good opening, logical ordering of events, and a sense of closure. Under Standard III, students were assessed on their mechanical and language skills, including

style and syntax, word choice, spelling, and punctuation. The point of this assessment was to provide us with a tool for evaluating how well the students understood the writing process. Were they able to guide and regulate their own learning with no teacher intervention? Could they take a standard prompt and develop this idea into a focused piece of expressive writing? Could they apply their knowledge of the writing process to their independent work? Could they use writing resources to self-evaluate and improve their own writing? Simply put, we were interested in seeing if the children could transfer their understanding of the writing process to a standardized writing context.

The three-day setting for this end-of-year assessment was during the regular forty-five-minute block for writers' workshop. The same prompt was given to all first-, second-, and third-grade students. On day 1, the students were given the following prompt: "Write about a special time that you've had with your family or friend. This will be your first draft copy. I won't help you in any way because you already know so many ways to help yourself." The children were allowed to use the entire period to develop their topic. However, when the first draft was completed, the teacher filed it away for the next day's step. On day 2, the teacher passed out the first draft version and said, "Today, I want you to reread your first draft and revise and edit your work. You can use dictionaries, checklists, or other resources to help yourself. I won't help you in any way because you already know how to help yourself." After the children had completed this process, they attached their editing checklists or practice pages to their edited version and turned all materials in to the teacher. On day 3, the teacher passed out the writing, and she prompted, "Today, you will write your final version. Reread your story; then write your final copy. I won't help you because you know how to help yourself."

First-Grade Writers

Let's look at three examples of work by first-graders. In the first example, Asia takes the prompt about a special time with her family and develops an expressive story entitled "Candyland" (Figure 2.1a). She uses a writer's technique of heavy, bold lines to express her feelings of anger, and she applies her knowledge of repetitive text structure to create a story that resembles many of the books she has read. For a first-grade writer, Asia's piece shows a sophisticated attempt to produce a contrasting pattern of images ("And it made me feel ANGRY! But it was just a game"). Toward the

Figure 2.1a Edited draft of Asia's story (first grade).

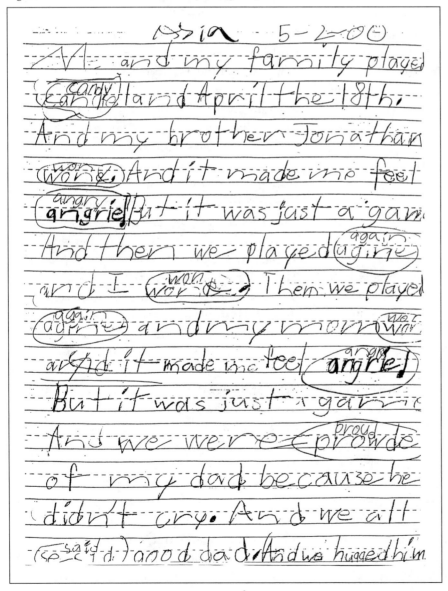

end of her story, she describes how they were all proud of her dad because he didn't cry. Although in the last two sentences, her story seems to fall apart, overall, Asia's writing is a strong piece with good qualities of a first-grade writer. In assessing her understanding of the writing process, Asia applies editing techniques (circling misspelled words); she uses the dictionary to correct all spelling errors (*angrie/angry; agine/again; prowde/proud; wone/won; sesid/said*); and she uses ending punctuation (exclamation mark, period) and capitalization with accuracy. Her final draft (Figure 2.1b) reflects all her revisions and corrections.

Figure 2.1b Final draft of Asia's story.

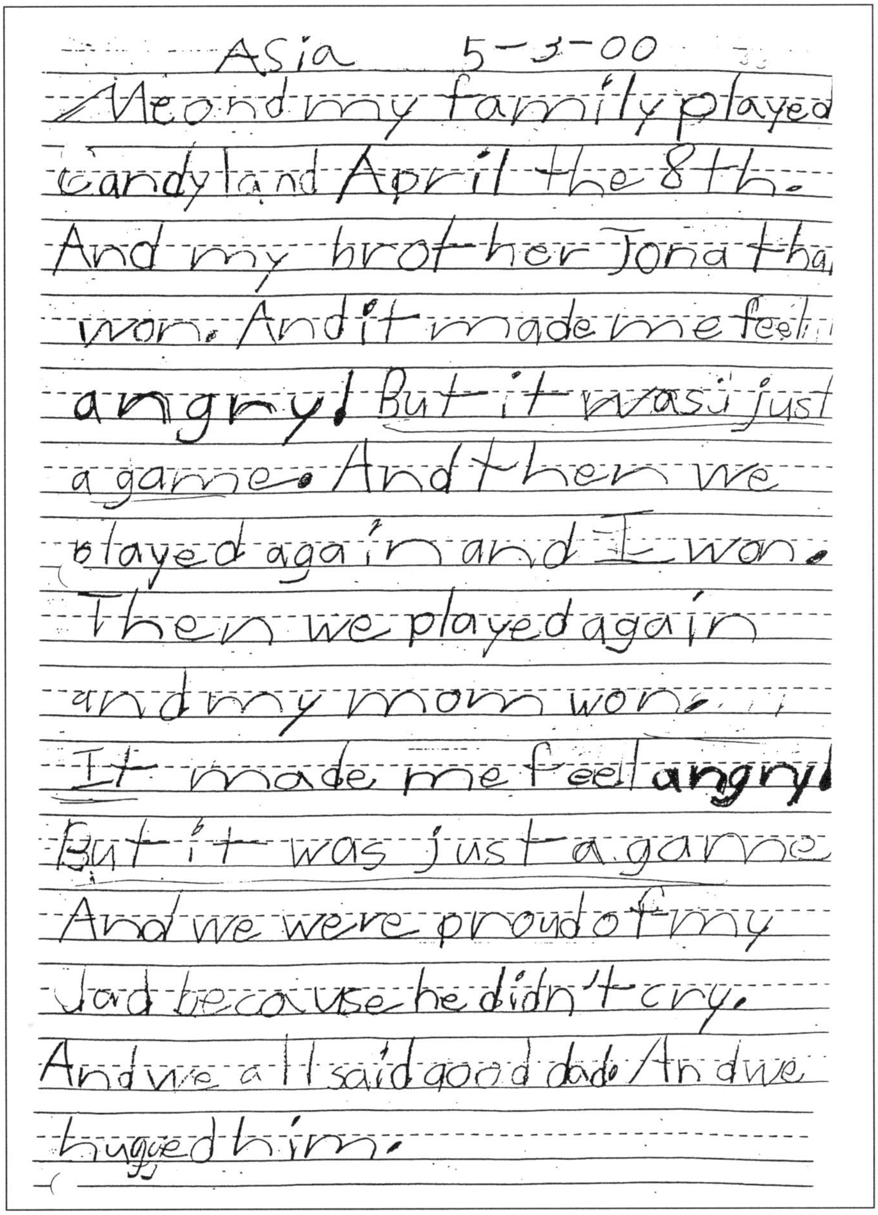

In the second example, Tharisha describes a special day at the park with her family (Figure 2.2). The story concentrates on a focal event, that is, playing hide-and-seek. Tharisha includes detailed sequences with repeated phrases ("I hid behind the tree. My mom hid behind the slide. Grandma hid behind the tall green grass") that build up to a culminating event ("Daddy said, Ready or not, here I come. So he found my mom first and my grandma next and me last"). She uses transitional words to create time flow in her story (*then, first, next, finally*). Her use of descriptive words (*tall green grass*) reflects her experience with book language. She concludes her story by telling about how she played the game with her thirteen-year-old brother. In her final statement, she revisits the intention of the story—to describe a special day with her family. For a first-grade writer, Tharisha shows a good understanding of writing purpose, and she knows how to develop a topic, add details, and sustain the idea throughout her piece. In the area of mechanics, Tharisha uses hyphens in *hide-and-seek*, a form of punctuation that we might not expect to see in first-grade writing. This can also be said of her accurate use of subjective pronouns (*my family and I*) in her first draft. In her edited version, she circles words, corrects *saed/said*, and uses her practice page (not shown) to try out several spellings for unknown words. These behaviors indicate that Tharisha understands the writing process and is able to write a well-focused story without teacher assistance.

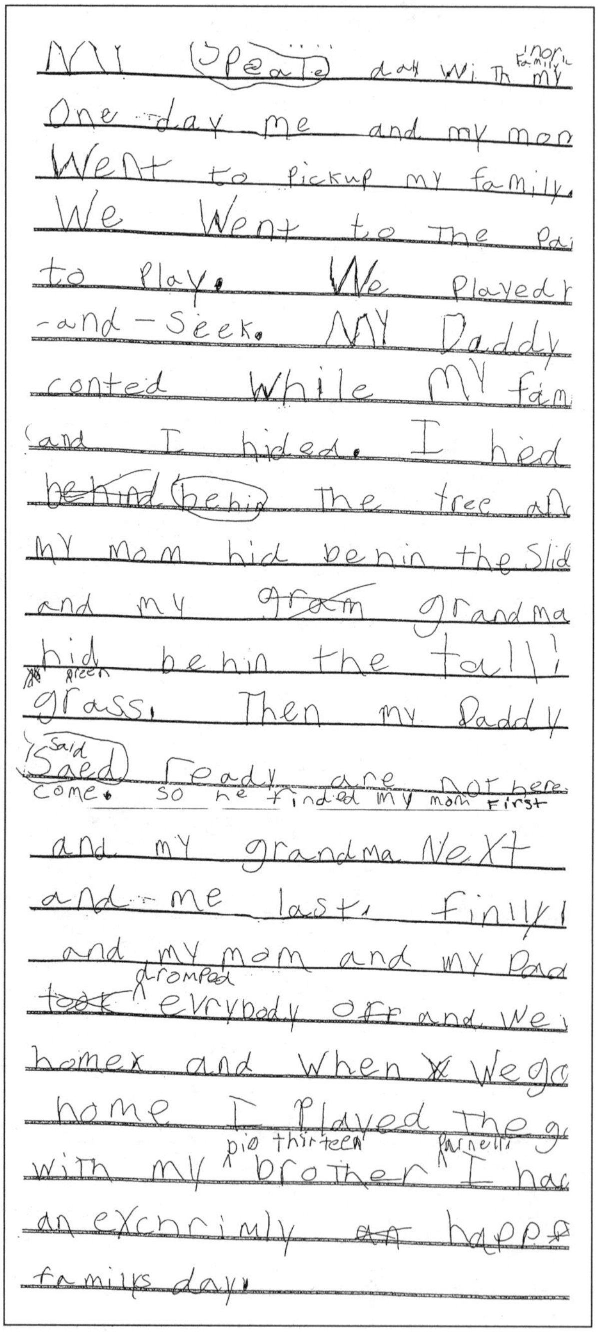

In the third example, Anna takes the topic of a special time and develops an expressive story about a skiing trip with her family (Figure 2.3). In her edited draft, she circled words that did not look right to her and self-corrected most of them. Her writing reflects her understanding of narrative text; she has a beginning, middle, and ending; and she uses details to expand upon her topic. Anna's writing is a nice example of how the voices of

Figure 2.2 Edited draft of Tharisha's story (first grade).

young writers can creep into their writing. This is characterized by writing that sounds like speech written down. In Anna's case, it is almost like a sideline conversation—her personal comments—that she interjects into the

Figure 2.3 Final draft of Anna's story (first grade).

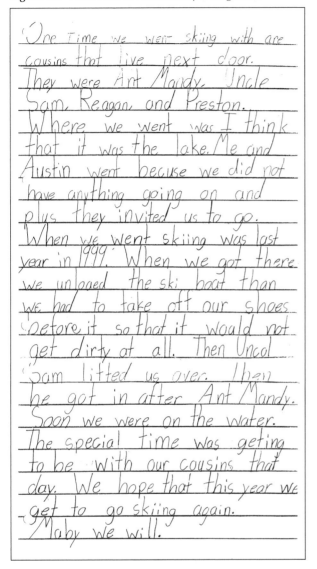

One Time we went skiing with are cousins that live next door. They were Ant Mandy, Uncle Sam, Reagan, and Preston. Where we went was I think that it was the lake. Me and Austin went because we did not have anything going on and plus they invited us to go. When we went skiing was last year in 1999. When we got there we unloaed the ski boat than we had to take off our shoes before it so that it would not get dirty at all. Then Uncol Sam lifted us over. Then he got in after Ant Mandy. Soon we were on the water. The special time was geting to be with our cousins that day. We hope that this year we get to go skiing again. Maby we will.

the year, the students were given the prompt "Write about a special time you've had with your family or friend." On the second- and third-grade rubrics (see Appendix A), writing criteria are slightly adjusted to reflect students' experience and knowledge with the writing process. For instance, on Standard II (audience and writing purposes), first-grade students are expected to include an opening sentence, but by third grade the students are assessed on their ability to develop good leads. A similar shift occurs in concluding the story: in first grade a sense of closure is appropriate, but by third grade students are expected to summarize their stories with a more interesting ending. This implies that knowledge of the writing process develops through meaningful and relevant practice over an extended period of time. In other words, in the primary grades, this is a case of becoming a better writer by practicing daily habits of writing.

Katie is a second-grade writer from a writers' workshop classroom. She builds on the prompt of a special time by describing a writing contest that she entered (Figure 2.4). She composes a lead section that establishes the theme of the story. In contrast to early writers (who generally write a single sentence or two), Katie's lead includes an opening sentence and dialogue. ("My class was reading a book. Then Mr. Barnhill said, 'We are going to enter a contest. It will be fun. You have to write a story with five pages and one hundred words'"). Her voice comes through in her writing ("I had fun writing. Not to brag but I think it was good") and is documented in her style of composing; for instance, she uses a range of sentence lengths, dialogue, transitional words, students' names, reactionary phrases, and a variety of punctuation. Katie uses words to communicate emotions ("I was ready to jump up!" "And that's when all the excitement fell out of me"). Her text has the characteristics of a story, with a beginning, middle, and ending,

story line ("Where we went was, I think that it was the lake. Me and Austin went because we did not have anything going on and plus they invited us to go"). She uses transitional words and adds a conclusion that focuses on the topic of a special day with her cousins.

Second- and Third-Grade Writers

Now let's look at the writing performance of second- and third-grade students. At the end of

Figure 2.4 Katie's story (second grade).

A Special Time
by
Katie

My class was reading a book. Then Mr. Barnhill said, "We are going to enter a contest." "It will be fun." "You have to write a story with five pages and one hundred words." I wrote mine. "It was called, "The Baby." I had fun writing it. Not to brag But I think it was good.

And last week we went to the multi purpose bilding. I didn't know what we were doing. First they said how proud they were of Mr. Smith for keeping the secret. He knew why we were there. Then they told us about it. It was the winners of the reading rainbow contest and water works contest. Isic Jumper won 3rd place in the water works

contest. I knew I wouldn't win that. Then they said, in second grade, She won state wide in the reading rainbow contest. I got exided. So did Ms. Barnhill. I was ready to jump up! Katie — I almost did jump. Then they said, Brook Davis. And thats when all the exitment fell out of me. I was upset.

So was Ms. Barnhill. I was happy for Katie I geuss. Her story was called, The Day I Got The Hicups. It must have ben better than The Baby. I am still dissapointed though.

including a sense of suspense that builds up to the announcement of the winner in the writing contest. In the area of mechanics, Katie shows knowledge of punctuation and grammar. On the writing rubric, Katie's overall piece meets the requirements for a proficient second-grade writer.

Darren, a third-grader, introduces the topic of a special time with his dad by establishing the scene for a frog gigging trip:

> One dark and cloudy night my dad and I went frog gigging in my Uncle David's pond. The pond was not just any old kind of pond. It was a special place for my dad and me to spend time together doing what we both love to do . . . frog gigging! The frogs love the pond, I think because of the tall spiny weeds for them to hide in when danger appears, the huge rocks for them to leap about on and the tremendous amount of crickets and bugs that swarm the top of the water.
>
> This night was no different. My dad came in from work late and said, "How about a trip to Uncle David's pond tonight?" I jumped up with excitement and headed for the garage to gather our spears, flashlight and buckets. Then dad and I hopped in the truck and drove to the pond. When we arrived the crickets were chirping, "chirp, chirp" and the frogs were croaking loudly. I could hardly wait to spear the first frog. Dad and I crept quietly toward the water shining our flashlights along the way. Finally, we were at the pond. I spotted two huge frogs on a rock. I wasted no time. I lifted up my spear and aimed it right toward the biggest frog. Whew . . . "Got him," I yelled. Dad gigged one and I gigged three! We ended up with twelve frog legs to take home that night.
>
> Going to my uncle's pond with my dad is a special time for me that I will never forget. I will always remember everything about our frog gigging trips and I know we will always go there as long as the frogs are still around.

In his opening paragraph, he uses words to create images of a special kind of pond ("not just any old kind of pond") where frogs are plentiful. He adds supporting details that describe the special nature of the pond ("tall spiny weeds for them to hide in when danger appears, huge rocks for them to leap about on and the tremendous amount of crickets and bugs that swarm the top of the water"). It is clear that Darren understands his topic, for his words provide a rich setting for a successful frog gigging trip. His voice is clear throughout his piece; for instance, he includes a variety of sentences, enthusiasm for the topic, effective use of dialogue, strong verbs, solid nouns, and rich descriptions. Furthermore, his writing reveals an understanding of paragraph structure: in his concluding paragraph, he revisits the topic of his writing and ends with closing statements that tie his piece together. Darren's final draft reflects proficiency in areas of punctuation, capitalization, and grammar. On the writing rubric, Darren exceeds the standard for a proficient third-grade writer.

Informal Assessments of Second- and Third-Grade Writers

In the previous section, we used a standardized assessment to provide us with valuable information on students' understanding of the writing process. In this section, we look at examples of informal writing assessments. Appendix B provides two forms that teachers can use with second- and third-grade students. First, the informal writing checklist provides teachers with an assessment tool that enables them to study children's writing development over time, including their ability to write texts in different genres (autobiography, biography, report, tall tale, folk tale, fairy tale, mystery, letter, note, directions, instructions, recipe, story retelling, innovation, and poetry). The second form is an example of a text guide—in this case, for tall tales—that can provide students with a temporary scaffold for composing (and evaluating) their own genre writings. Let's look at two examples of students' work from a third-grade classroom.

In the first example, Jackie's draft version of a tall tale (Figure 2.5) indicates her understanding of the writing process; for instance, she rearranges her text to clarify meaning, inserts words and phrases, revises word choices, and circles words that do not look right. In the area of mechanics, Jackie shows proficiency with capitalization, punctuation, pronoun usage, and subject-verb agreement. In language areas, Jackie uses a variety of sentence structures. In her first draft, she does not attend to paragraph structure, but in her final draft (not shown), which resulted from a teacher conference, Jackie indicated that she is aware of this skill.

A secondary goal of this assessment is to study how well the student applies knowledge

Figure 2.5 Jackie's tall tale (third grade).

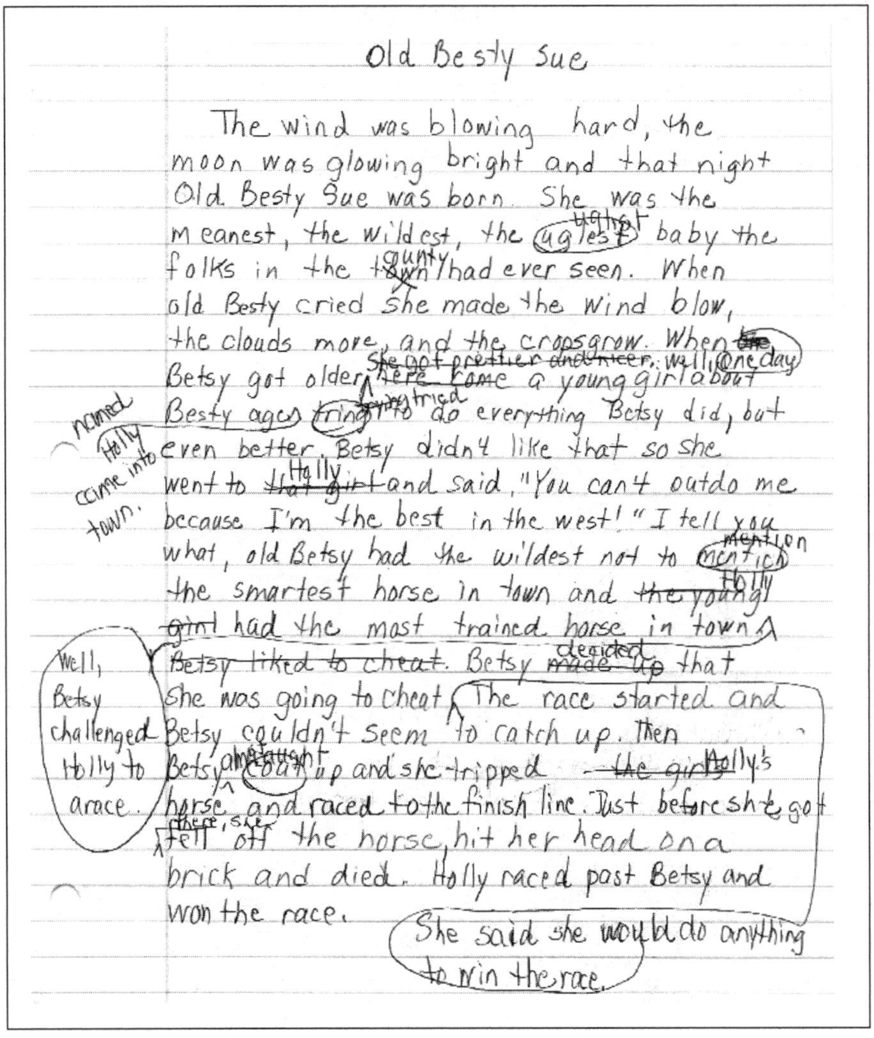
Old Besty Sue

The wind was blowing hard, the
moon was glowing bright and that night
Old Besty Sue was born. She was the
meanest, the wildest, the uglest (ugliest) baby the
folks in the ~~town~~ county had ever seen. When
old Besty cried she made the wind blow,
the clouds move, and the cropsgrow. When ~~the~~
Betsy got older, She got ~~prettier and nicer~~. Well, one day ~~here came~~ a young girl about
Besty ages ~~tring~~ trying to do everything Betsy did, but
even better. Betsy didn't like that so she
went to ~~that girl~~ Holly and said, "You can't outdo me
because I'm the best in the west!" I tell you
what, old Betsy had the wildest not to mention
the smartest horse in town and ~~the young~~ Holly
~~girl~~ had the most trained horse in town.
~~Betsy liked to cheat.~~ Betsy ~~made up~~ decided that
she was going to cheat. The race started and
Betsy couldn't seem to catch up. Then
Betsy almost caught up and she tripped ~~the girl~~ Holly's
horse and raced to the finish line. Just before she got
there, she fell off the horse, hit her head on a
brick and died. Holly raced past Betsy and
won the race.
She said she would do anything
to win the race.

named Holly came into town.

Well, Betsy challenged Holly to arace.

of genre to independent writing. Thus, teachers have prepared text guides that students can use to organize and evaluate different forms of writing. Jackie has written a tall tale entitled "Old Betsy Sue." She includes many of the characteristics associated with this genre. For instance, in her lead sentences, she uses words to create an image of the night that Old Betsy Sue was born. ("The wind was blowing hard, the moon was glowing bright, and that night Old Betsy Sue was born"). Jackie displays an understanding for how exaggerations can be used for developing character traits: "When Old Betsy cried, she made the wind blow, the clouds move, and the crops grow." She uses phrases that create an atmosphere of a storyteller sitting on a porch while spinning a yarn of exaggerated events ("I tell you what," "not to mention"). Here, Jackie meets the criteria for writing a tall tale, yet as her story continues, it begins to lose its quality as a tall tale. With more experience in this genre, Jackie will acquire greater proficiency in writing this type of story.

Now let's look at Mahdi's writing sample of a tall tale, a final draft of a story that he composed in writers' workshop:

The Tale of Jack Green

One stormy night a baby was born in a one room house in Texas. He could pick up one hundred pounds with one hand. When he cried he would scare a bear one hundred miles away. His name was Jack Green. Jack was as strong as three hundred bears and could run so fast that he could beat four hundred cheetahs. Jack was the strongest man in Texas.

Jack learned about cowboys and he was the best cowboy across the state. Then he met a bull. "I bet I can ride that bull just like a horse."

"Do you want to ride that bull?" asked a stranger. "That's the wildest bull in the west and nobody can ride it."

"I want to ride it today," Jack said.

The bull did not buck Jack. Jack made the bull his friend. One day a girl was riding a bear and her name was Sue Blue. She was the wildest girl in the west. Her horse's name was Lightning. Sue and Jack got married.

Jack had to do a pounds test to see who was the strongest man in the world. The first one was 50 pounds, then 60 pounds, then 100 pounds, then 1000 pounds and Jack won the test. Sue was as happy as a cat.

Sue had a fight with a lion and she won. Sue and Jack went east to Little Rock, and on the way, they met Paul Bunyan. Paul was going to Texas in the South. Sue, Jack, and Paul were going across the world, but Sue left Jack. Jack was mad at Paul and he had a fight with Paul and won.

Jack went to Texas. There was a flood and Jack had to do something, so he got a big bucket and put the water in it and poured it in the hole and he made a lake. It was the biggest lake in the world. He saved everyone's life and he was made the smartest man in Texas.

In contrast to Jackie's story, Mahdi shows a better understanding of the tall tale genre. For instance, he uses exaggerations to illustrate the size and strength of the characters ("scare a bear one hundred miles away," lift 1000 pounds, fight a lion and win, stop a flood with a bucket, and make the biggest lake in the world). In his setting, he places his characters in real locations (Texas, Little Rock), thus bringing truth and fantasy together to create a tall tale. In his piece, Mahdi describes how the character deals with hardships by using his strength and size to overcome challenges. Based on this writing sample, Mahdi understands this genre form; as he reads more, his skills with writing tall tales will improve. A filled-in checklist for Mahdi's story is shown in Figure 2.6.

Figure 2.6 Checklist for Mahdi's tall tale (third grade). Appendix B provides a blank form.

1. What is the title of the tall tale? _The Tale of Jack Green_

2. Describe the setting? In what country or region does it take place? _Stormy night in Texas - Went to Little Rock_

3. Who is the hero/heroine? _Jack Green_

4. Describe the qualities of hero/heroine. _Strong, fast, big Smartest man in Texas_

5. Who are the other characters in the story? _Sue Blue, Paul Bunyan_

6. Describe the qualities of the other characters. _Sue - Wildest girl in West_

7. What was the hardship to overcome in the story? _riding th bull - Stopping the flood in Texas._

8. How was the hardship solved? _He made the bull his friend - In Texas he got a bucket of water and poured it in a hole and made a lake._

9. What exaggerations are used in the tall tale? _Strong as 300 bears - run fast as 400 cheetahas - lifted a thousand pounds - made a lake_

Benchmark Writing Behaviors

Kindergarten Writing

During literacy team meetings (see Dorn, French, and Jones 1998; Dorn and Soffos 2001a), teachers have analyzed children's writing samples over time, and they've identified benchmark behaviors for proficiency at different grade levels. Let's take a look at some examples of proficient writing for kindergarten to third-grade students. At the end of the kindergarten year, teachers can expect students to:

- Generate topics and lists for writing
- Understand that writing should make sense
- Write a narrative that includes three or four events in order
- Produce writing that uses some of the words and phrases from read-aloud books
- Write a reaction to a story
- Maintain a focus for writing about a topic

- Read their own writing to others (soon after the writing is completed, they can still remember the message)
- Write initial sounds and some ending sounds to represent words (semiphonetic stage of spelling)
- Leave spaces between words
- Experiment with punctuation (e.g., use periods or exclamation marks throughout their writing)

Rachel's writing (Figure 2.7) meets the proficiency standard for a kindergarten writer at the end of the year. Here, she responds to an informational book, *Where Are the Eggs?*, a text she has read in her kindergarten guided reading group. In her piece, Rachel maintains a focus for the story and includes specific details that relate to the topic (mothers and their eggs). In the area of spelling development, Rachel exceeds proficiency for her grade level. She writes six different high-frequency words accurately (*is, in, the, are, for, looking*), and her attempts to spell unknown words can be classified as being at the phonetic stage (*Muther, trtl, sea, hr, chikin, fiding, bloow, brd, srching, fluminggo*). She understands the concept of space and shows an awareness of capitalization (*Muther*) and ending punctuation (she adds a period in two places—after *feeding yard* and at the end of her story). Rachel has developed important skills and strategies for writing; furthermore, she has acquired a habit of writing.

Figure 2.7 A writing sample from a proficient kindergartner.

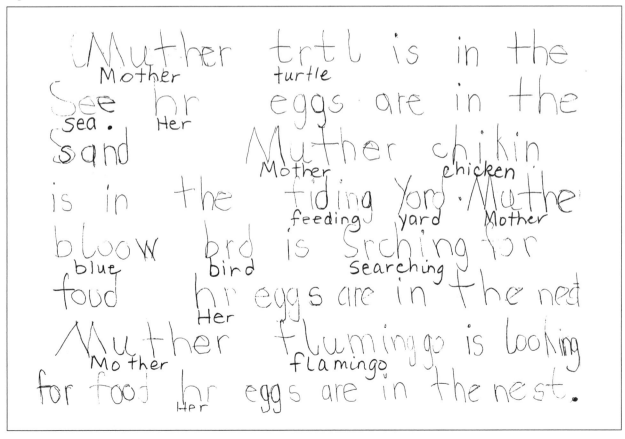

First-Grade Writing

The first-grade teachers identified the following behaviors as goals for first-grade writers. The checklist provides teachers with a road map for planning focused mini-lessons. By the end of the first-grade year, teachers can expect the writer to

- Use a topic sentence that grabs the reader's attention
- Organize texts according to beginning, middle, and ending parts
- Include supporting details
- Write informational texts on known topics
- Demonstrate an awareness of how descriptive language can be used to add interesting details to a story
- Use capitalization and punctuation correctly most of the time
- Think about how words look visually and use this knowledge to problem-solve on unknown words
- Write high-frequency words with ease
- Use a dictionary to check spellings of unknown words
- Demonstrate an awareness of how a thesaurus can help with word meanings in writing a story

Madison, a first-grade writer, is well on her way to meeting proficiency in these benchmark areas. Her December writing sample (Figure 2.8) is a first draft of an informational text that outlines the steps for building a snowman. She uses a topic sentence to introduce the theme and includes five specific steps in sequence for building the snowman. Madison's voice comes through in her piece, as she tells the reader, "I hope next time you will get it right. That's what I did last year and I had a fun time." Her use of transitional words (*last year, then, also, after that*) indicates her understanding of time elements for explaining the order of events. In the area of mechanics, Madison spells high-frequency words correctly; she makes good phonetic approximations for unknown words; she circles several words that do not look right to her (*stec/sticks; a raned/around; hed/head; rily/really*); and she uses a simple dictionary to self-correct some of these words (*hat, next, how, what*). Madison is in a writers' workshop classroom, and she views writing as a natural part of her day. Based on this sample, we can assume that she will meet the proficiency standards for writing performance by the end of her first-grade year.

Second-Grade Writing

By second grade, students should be able to sustain their attention for longer periods of writing. They can spell most high-frequency words automatically, and they have acquired a repertoire of strategies for spelling unknown words. Their understanding of the writing process will continue to develop as they work on longer pieces of writing and gain more experience with various genres. Classroom teachers have identified the following benchmark behaviors as evidence of writing proficiency for second-graders:

- Stay focused on a topic
- Use dialogue effectively
- Develop settings and characters with richer details
- Write longer texts with multiple problems
- Use figurative language, similes, and metaphors
- Use text maps and guides to plan and evaluate writing
- Create good lead sentences that grab the reader's attention
- Show awareness of paragraph organization for grouping ideas
- Use editing resources to check on spellings (dictionary, checklists, wall charts)

Figure 2.8 A writing sample by a proficient first-grader.

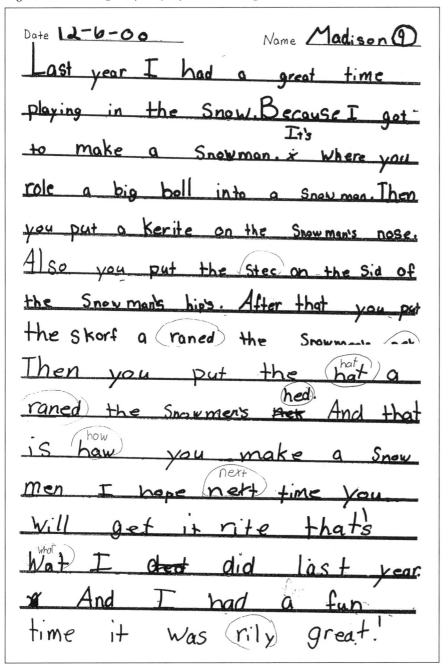

- Use a thesaurus to revise word meanings
- Show awareness of comma usage
- Use pronouns appropriately most of the time

Molly, a second-grade student, meets proficiency for writing an informational text. Her piece is a published version that includes accurate details and precise information about frogs

(Figure 2.9). She has written two pages of well-organized text that reveal her understanding of this format. She includes an opening sentence that introduces her topic ("I am going to tell you about the life cycle about frogs!") and a closing section that concludes her writing ("I sure had a great time learning about the life cycle of frogs. Did you? I hope so!"). Her knowledge of content and text organization is adequate for a second-grade writer. Since this is her published version, her spellings and punctuation are accurate. Molly is in a writers' workshop classroom, and she understands the processes of planning, first draft, revising, editing, final draft, and publication. For this piece, she used a variety of writing tools to help herself, including an informational guide to organize her writing, editing checklists, and classroom resources (dictionaries and reference books).

Third-Grade Writing

By the end of third grade, children have grown considerably as writers. They understand the importance of their audience; and their knowledge of the writing craft has improved with practice. In many of the benchmark areas, third-grade writers are similar to second-grade writers. The major difference is that third-graders have acquired an extra year of experience, resulting in their ability to produce longer texts with richer content and vocabulary. Also, these students have become more efficient at revising their pieces, including cut-and-paste techniques for adding sentences and moving around paragraphs. They carry a writer's log around with them and record notes and ideas as they occur. Some benchmark behaviors of third-grade writers include

- Write longer texts with more complex language patterns

- Create texts that include chapters, tables of contents, and diagrams
- Use paragraphs to organize text
- Use figurative language, similes, metaphors with greater ease
- Use vocabulary and phrases that stimulate images in the minds of the reader
- Use lead sentences that pull the reader into the text
- Use classroom references and writing tools independently
- Apply standard criteria to self-evaluate work

Following are two samples of writing that exceed the criteria for proficiency at the end of third grade. The first is a poem entitled "Wisteria Vine."

Wisteria Vine
A pretty wisteria vine grows in my yard.
The flowers are fragrant.
Soft, purple and silky, but the vine is very hard.
When I'm walking with my dog or a friend,
Its fragrant scent is brought to me by the wind.
I feel as though it were blooming just for me.
That beautiful wisteria vine growing up a tree.

In this piece, Elizabeth uses words to create images of smell ("fragrant scent is brought to me by the wind") and touch ("soft, purple and silky, but the vine is very hard"). She understands how phrases can be arranged to create a smooth rhythmic quality that is associated with poetic writing. Elizabeth is an avid writer, and she carries her writer's log with her everywhere she goes. She records the smallest impressions of sound, sight, and touch. When she writes poetry, she uses sensory words to evoke rich images in the minds of her readers. In a second piece by Elizabeth, she writes a mystery in journal form, based on the adventures of Sherlock Holmes. Here, we have

Figure 2.9 A writing sample by a proficient second-grader.

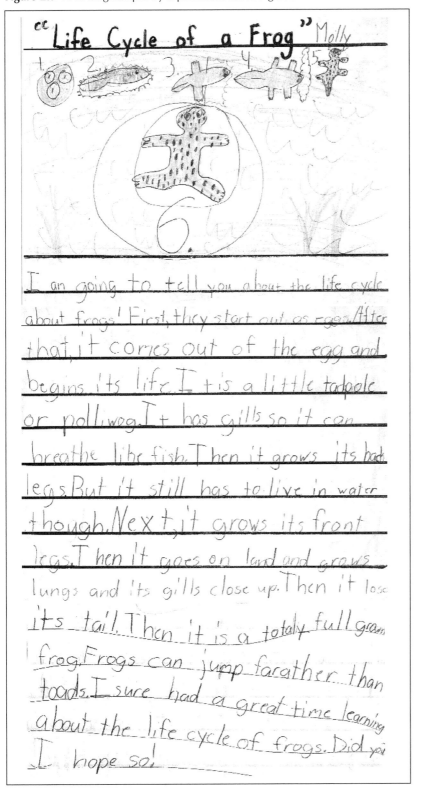

included one entry from her journal to illustrate her understanding of the writing craft.

The Journal of Elizabeth Holmes, 1921

The murder took place in a large city in a valley in Egypt. There had been a terrorist attack recently and many people had been killed. I am Detective Elizabeth Holmes and my assistant is Tiffan. The mystery I am about to solve is the Mystery of the Silver Perfume Bottle.

The mystery started when there was a terrorist attack at the Cairo Airport. One of the people murdered was a lantern maker. Someone had told me that the murderer was one of the man's protectors. It was also said that one of the man's ancestors had been one of King Tut's subjects and that the man knew where King Tut's tomb was located. The man was rich and the heir to a fortune when his uncle died. His protector had murdered him to get all of the money that he had just inherited. I decided to search his house. It was there that I found a peculiar looking little silver perfume bottle. It had perfume in it. I sprayed some on. Along with a musty scent, a note floated out. It had been written by the lantern maker. It said to keep his servant Roli undercover because he had vowed to kill the lantern maker. The note also said that King Tut's tomb was in the Valley of the Kings!

I quickly wrote Howard Carter and told him about the tomb. Later in 1922, King Tut's tomb was discovered.

She creates a setting that is based on realistic events (a terrorist attack at the Cairo airport); she includes real people in her story (King Tut, Howard Carter); and she develops a mystery around a known happening (the discovery of King Tut's tomb). In both of Elizabeth's writing samples, she shows an ability to use language in expressive ways.

Three Modes of Writing

An important goal of writing proficiency is the student's ability to write for different audiences and purposes. This means that teachers must provide children with a range of writing experiences. Earlier, we shared a writing checklist that includes a section for documenting children's writing performance on various types of text (see Appendix B). For teachers, this checklist helps to ensure that we are providing our students with opportunities to learn how to write in different forms. In classrooms, we emphasize three modes of writing, which include the expressive, transactional, and poetic forms (Briton 1970). Here, we share writing examples from kindergarten to third-grade classrooms that illustrate these three forms.

Expressive Writing

This writing is personal writing, so it often sounds like speech written down. It is the easiest form of writing for the beginning writer because it is based on the child's own language and experiences. Students should feel comfortable with this form of writing before they move on to the transactional and poetic forms. Expressive forms of writing include journal writing, personal letters, and narrative stories that revolve around the writer's life (what he likes, what happens to him, where he goes). Figures 2.10–2.13 show examples of expressive writing from primary classrooms.

First, we have a kindergarten sample written by Brooke, who tells a story about Ryan's lost tooth. Brooke's topic is interesting and relevant, and she includes herself and three of her classmates in her story. The next example is an edited draft of Maribeth's story, which was composed during writers' workshop in her first-grade classroom. Here, Maribeth expresses her feelings about a tornado that

Figure 2.10 Expressive writing—kindergarten.

Ryan last his tooth
we loot with madi gass
Allie sad hier it is
But it wus a rok
we wer wrid
I sad I hap we fid it
finul Rebecca fad it
I'm gad we fid it To: Ryan
From Brooke

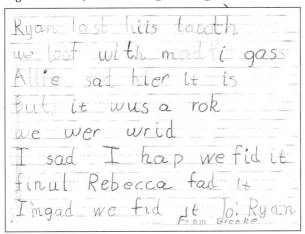

Figure 2.11 Expressive writing—first grade.

One night there was a bad
storm we were all scared.
Tornados came. My brother is scared
of a (tornado) practice but when the real one
comes my brother goes, "When is the
tornado coming. I was the one scared.
I had pillows on top of my head.
I was in the hall because the hall had no
My dad saw the tornado.
The clouds were very low.
But the tornado was up in the sky.
I was very very very
very scared. The End. We could
bearly eat supper then we took a bath
very fast. My mum patted me on the back
it comft me down a little bit but...
...Not much. I hope a tornado never comes again.
The End

Figure 2.12 Expressive writing—second grade.

when Me and my baking cookies it was fun.
We baked sugar cookies. We had
to put in sugar, eggs, butter,
milk. Then We got the big bowl and
the wooden spoon to stirer the
cookies. Then we put them in the oven. We
let them cook. We put the stoen
on 350 the gries. I could
smell them in the stoen. First,
We let them cool... them down.
Scound we scape the cookeis
off the pan and put them on a plate.
Next we put spinkcel and crem on
Then we gave some to our
niobrys and friends. Then we ate
some. They were desciloon. I
had ate 4 cookies becuse they
was good. The cookies was
very chewy and they was warm as
the sping. I love cookies!

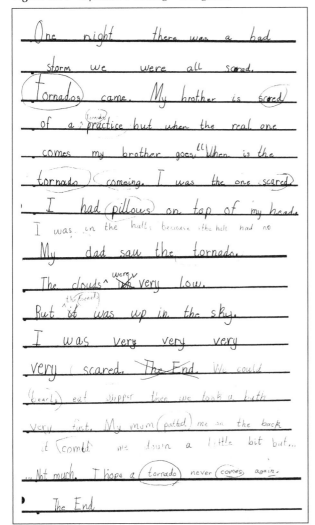

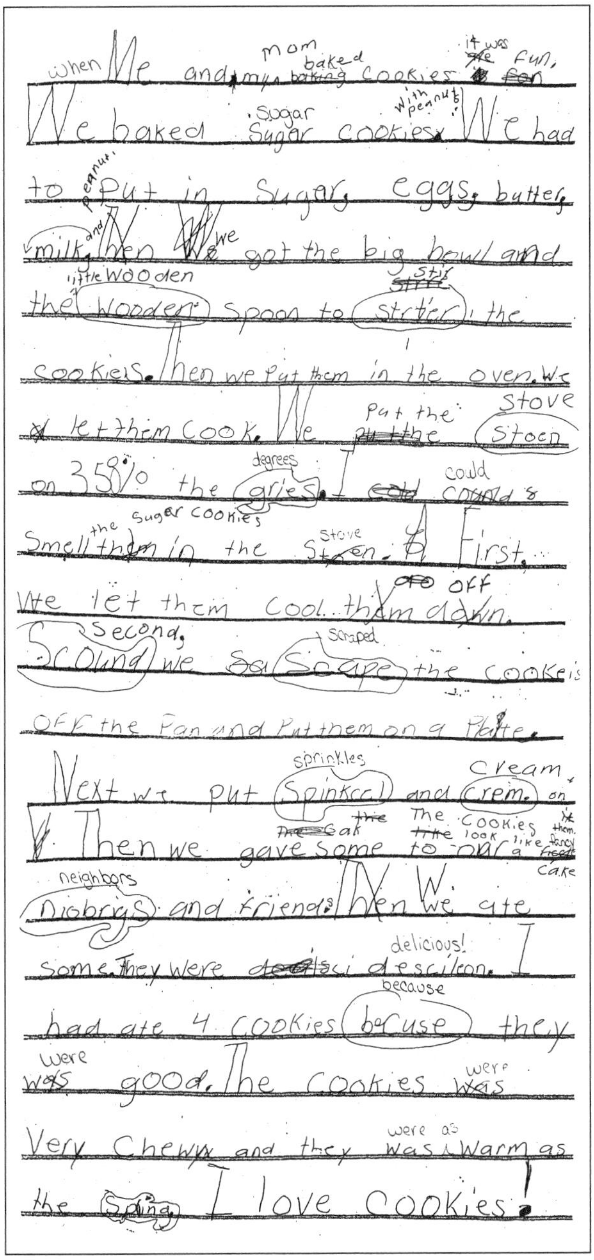

Figure 2.13 Expressive writing—third grade.

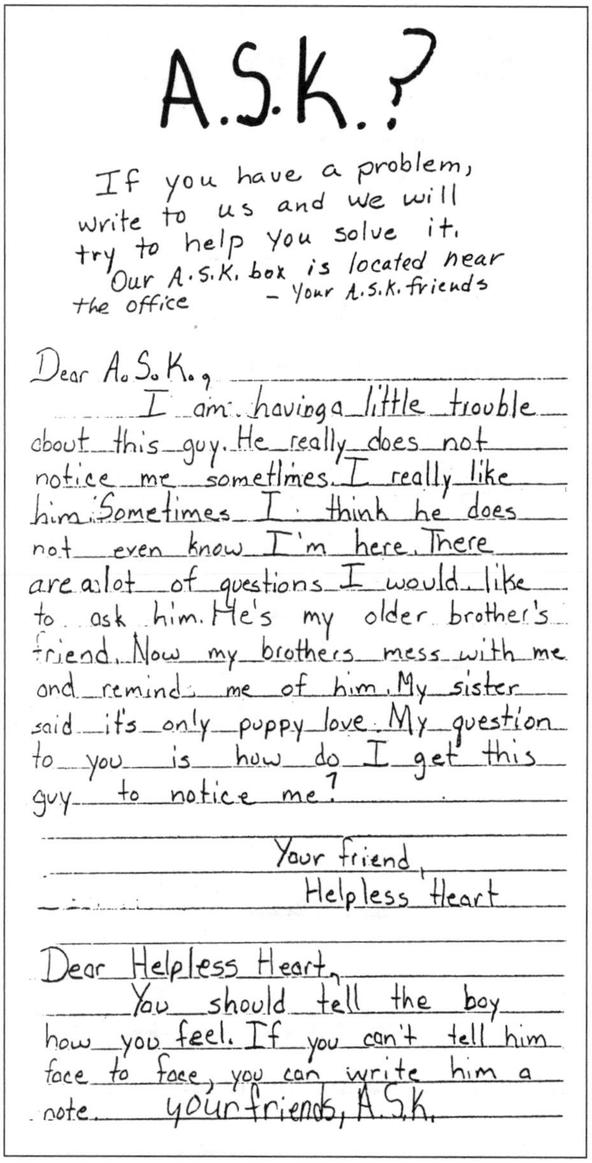

A.S.K.?

If you have a problem,
write to us and we will
try to help you solve it.
Our A.S.K. box is located near
the office   — Your A.S.K. friends

Dear A.S.K.,
        I am having a little trouble
about this guy. He really does not
notice me sometimes. I really like
him. Sometimes I think he does
not even know I'm here. There
are a lot of questions I would like
to ask him. He's my older brother's
friend. Now my brothers mess with me
and remind me of him. My sister
said it's only puppy love. My question
to you is how do I get this
guy to notice me?

                        Your friend,
                        Helpless Heart

Dear Helpless Heart,
        You should tell the boy
how you feel. If you can't tell him
face to face, you can write him a
note.   your friends, A.S.K.

advice. Each of these examples illustrates the expressive writing.

Transactional Writing

This writing is explicit writing. The purpose is to communicate information in clear, precise, and accurate language. This form of writing can present a challenge to a young writer who has limited knowledge of a particular topic. When teachers introduce transactional writing to children, they ensure that the writing topic is a familiar and comfortable one. Some examples of transactional writing include lists, signs, directions, recipes, reports, maps, and recording instructions for solving problems in spelling, math, and other work areas. When teachers work with children in creating literacy checklists, they are exposing them to the functional quality of transactional writing. In Figures 2.14–2.17, we have four examples of transactional writing. In the first example, Timothy, a kindergarten student, writes a note to the teacher and deposits it in the class "Tattle Box." The note is functional and purposeful, that is, in Timothy's case, to tell on Austin, who pushed him off the gray monkey bars. In the second example, Zacoby, a first-grader, gives directions for how to cook hot dogs. It is clear that he understands the recipe form because his writing includes the appropriate ingredients and a logical sequence of directions for preparing the hot dogs. Next, Thomas, a second-grader, reports on the planet Mars; and James, a third-grader, writes about alligators. Both of these samples include accurate information about a topic that the students have independently researched.

Poetic Writing

This type of literary writing is more concerned with the role of language for expressing images

had passed over her home the previous weekend. In the third example, Brittany, a second-grade student, composes a story based on baking cookies with her mom. She uses words to recreate the experience in chronological order. The final example is taken from an after-school writing club in an inner-city school. Here, a student has written a personal letter to the editor, who has responded to her with personal

Figure 2.14 Transactional writing—kindergarten.

A llstin

pusHt me

Off the

eray muncy

bare

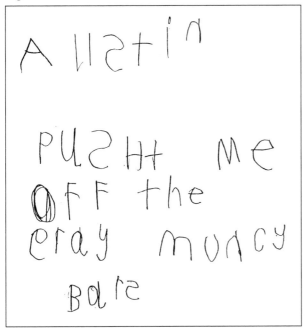

Figure 2.15 Transactional writing—first grade.

Hot Dogs

mustard meat

ketchup Buns

First put Water

in a pan. Then I

cook it on The

Stove for a minute.

I put the meat in

the Bun. Then put

the mustard

and ketchup on

the meat. Eat it.

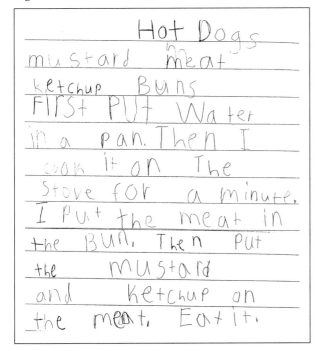

Figure 2.16 Transactional writing—second grade.

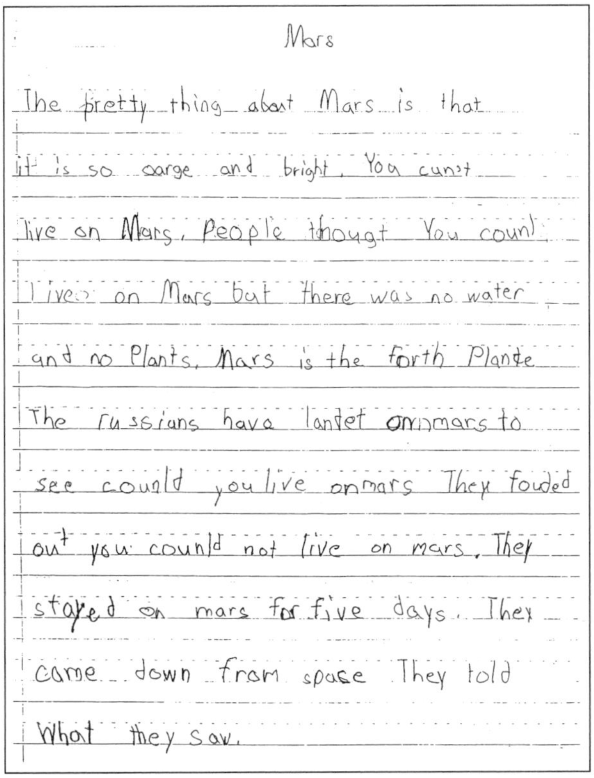

Mars

The pretty thing abat Mars is that

it is so oarge and bright. You cunst

live on Mars. People thougt You counl

lives on Mars but there was no water

and no Plants. Mars is the forth Plante

The russians hava lantet onmars to

see counld youlive onmars They fouded

out you counld not live on mars. They

stayed on mars for five days. They

came down from space They told

What they saw.

Figure 2.17 Transactional writing—third grade.

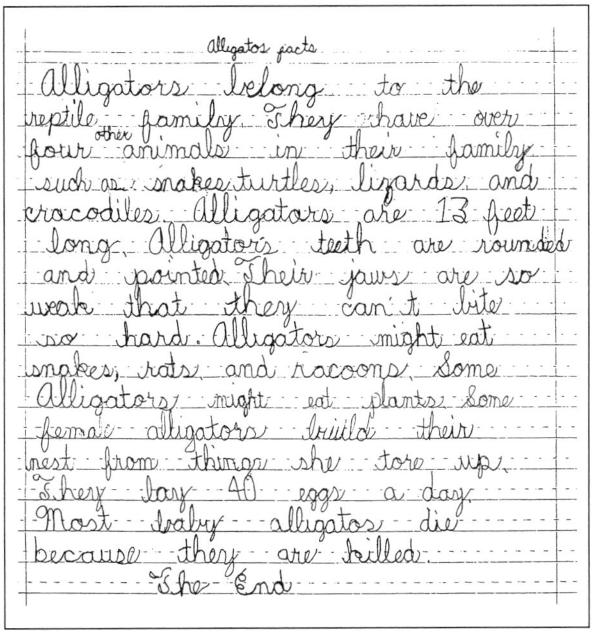

alligatos facts

Alligators belong to the

reptile family. They have over

four other animals in their family

such as: snakes, turtles, lizards, and

crocodiles. Alligators are 13 feet

long. Alligators teeth are rounded

and pointed. Their jaws are so

weak that they can't bite

so hard. Alligators might eat

snakes, rats, and racoons. Some

Alligators might eat plants. Some

female alligators build their

nest from things she tore up.

They lay 40 eggs a day.

Most baby alligatos die

because they are killed.

The End

and feelings. It requires the writer to understand how language is used to communicate a rich and descriptive message. When children read lots of books, they acquire the tools for writing in the poetic mode. At the emergent and early levels, during shared reading and writing experiences, teachers expose young children to literary language. Poetic writing requires that children understand the patterns of language, including text organization, sentence structures, word meanings, and figurative language. With this style of writing, children become more conscious of word choices for expressing their precise meanings. Some examples of this form of writing include poetry, story innovations, retellings, plays, and personal reactions to literature. In Figures 2.18–2.21, we have examples of poetic writing. In the first example, Matt, a kindergartner, reacts to *The Rainbow Fish* (Pfister 1992). In his literature response log, he records a simple retelling of the story. In the second example, Allison, a first-grade student, writes a more complete retelling of the story *The Great Big Enormous Turnip* (Oxenbury 1968). Next, Anna, a second-grade student, writes a personal

Figure 2.19 Poetic writing—first grade.

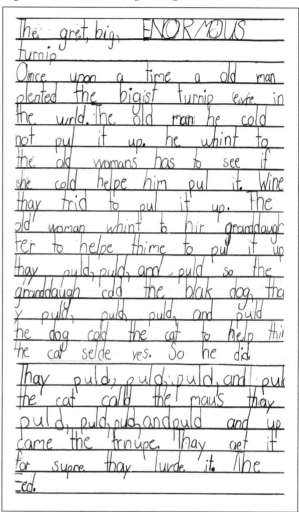

Figure 2.18 Poetic writing—kindergarten.

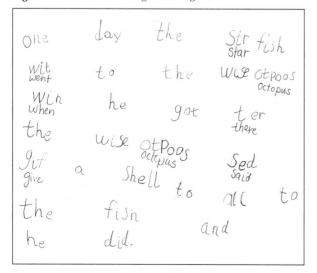

response to a story about the experiences of people who traveled to America on the *Mayflower*. In her text, she uses words to create images of crowded space and the difficulties of living on the ship. The final example shows a poem by Erin, a third-grader, in typed form. In her piece, she uses words to describe a feeling of bright colors, falling leaves, and tantalizing smells of food, all working together to produce a feeling of a crisp autumn day. In each example, the writers have used their knowledge of language to create texts of a literary nature.

Figure 2.20 Poetic writing—second grade.

If I was on the Mayflower I would try not to complain. But I would most of all try not to look down and get seasick. I bet down in that tiney space it would be heard to take all of the things that belong to you and 102 other people with all of their things that belong to them. I bet spending as many days as they did in such a tiney space would just make you sick from being scrunched for so many days. If I was in that tiney space and he said "land a hoye" I bet people would be jumping all over me. There is another thing I want to talk about. Way back then they did not have tooth brushes so they had to use a rag to clean their teeth and boy I would not like to do that at all. If I had to go to the pot I would try to hold it so I would not have to use a chamber pot. I am so glad I was not on the Mayflower.

Figure 2.21 Poetic writing—third grade.

Scene of Autumn

The hills are beautiful with green, brown, and orange
Down in the valley, it's raining leaves.
The wind tickles my nose and makes me sneeze.
Through windows you can smell turkey cooking.
You can see pie making.
I like to jump in the leaves
And draw pictures using the colors of autumn.

Closing Thoughts

In this chapter, we have shared how teachers assess children's writing for behavioral evidence of writing development. All the writing samples came from kindergarten to third-grade classrooms where writers' workshop is a daily occurrence. Based on ongoing observations of children's learning patterns, teachers design literacy opportunities that enable their students to reach their highest potential. In the next chapter, we continue to examine the link between teaching and learning as we discuss the role of writers' workshop in scaffolding young writers.

Organizing for Writers' Workshop

In Chapter 2, we discussed the writing progress of kindergarten through third-grade writers. Here, we explain the importance of writers' workshop for shaping the writing development of young children. When we look at children's writing, we should expect to see evidence of two kinds of learning:

- More stability and ease of using known information (fluency and automaticity)
- Conscious efforts to apply new learning (sustained attention and concentration)

Furthermore, if children's writing is not progressing, we must look at our own teaching. Are we providing children with daily opportunities to learn how to become a writer? Is our teaching mediating processing activity and promoting independence in our students? We believe that writers' workshop is a critical component of a primary curriculum for literacy.

What Is Writers' Workshop?

Writers' workshop is a literacy block where children learn the processes of how to write (Calkins 1986; Graves 1994). The teacher structures the time to ensure that children have an opportunity to plan, organize, and carry out writing projects. During writers' workshop, students learn how to select their own topics and develop these topics through multiple drafts. Thus, they acquire an understanding of the writing process.

Historically, the writing process has been associated with five stages of writing: prewriting, drafting, revising, editing, and publishing. These stages provide the writer (and teacher) with a good framework for developing a writing project.

Prewriting

The writer begins by identifying the purpose and audience for her writing. For instance, if she wants to write a letter to a friend inviting him to a birthday party, she will plan her writing based on a specific need to communicate this particular message. Basically, the prewriting stage is about planning, gathering, and organizing ideas for writing. This can occur as oral discussion or as written organizing with tools such as an outline, map, or notes.

Drafting

Now the writer begins to draft his ideas on paper. At this stage, the content is emphasized, rather than mechanics. Students are encouraged to transcribe their thoughts with fluency, thus keeping their focus on the development of their ideas. The drafting stage can consist of several attempts to construct an idea; for instance, a writer might draft different lead sentences to introduce his topic. The point here is that drafting is not restricted to a first copy of the entire paper; it can also include multiple drafts of particular sections of the paper, such as character development, good settings, interesting lead sentences, and catchy endings. Good writers use drafting as an important tool for organizing, reorganizing, and reflecting on the quality of their compositions. Thus, drafts can be numerous and messy.

Revising

Here, the writer rereads the message for clarity and best choice of words. He uses techniques such as carets (to add words or phrases), lines and crosses (to delete unnecessary information), circles with connecting lines (to move pieces of text to a new position), and cut-and-paste (to rearrange larger chunks of passage within the text). During revising, the writer shares his piece with listeners, who provide him with constructive feedback on the clearness of his message; also, listeners might offer suggestions for making the composition more interesting. A writer's piece can go through several revisions prior to final draft.

Editing

During editing, the writer proofreads her composition for mechanical mistakes, including spelling, grammar, and punctuation. She uses spelling tools to identify errors. For instance, she circles misspelled words, tries the spellings out several ways on a trial page, and uses the dictionary to correct spellings. In areas of grammar and punctuation, she applies her knowledge of language skills to edit as many errors as possible.

Publishing

If a writer decides to publish her work, she engages in a process of organizing the piece for a public audience. This means she must decide how to lay out the text in the most appealing way to the reader. If the piece is designed for a book, the writer must consider important organizational aspects, such as how much text to put on each page, when to include pictures to illustrate the text, how to design a title page, and how to bind the book in the most appropriate form. If the piece is a poem or report, the publication requirements can follow a different set of criteria. However, in all cases, published work has an obligation to the reader; thus, writers must develop an understanding of acceptable conventions for preparing writing for an audience.

To support children's understanding of the writing process, teachers can display a chart that outlines the steps of the writing process (see Appendix C), writing samples of different modes (Figure 3.1), and an exhibit of children's work (Figure 3.2).

Assessing Students' Writing

Teachers continually assess their students' writing by asking questions and studying writing behaviors. Here are some examples of questions that teachers might ask about their students' knowledge of the writing process.

Figure 3.1 Display of different modes of writing.

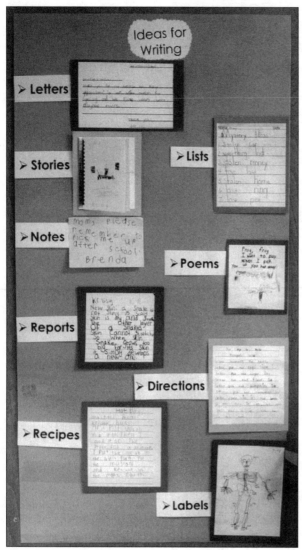

Prewriting and Drafting

Is the writer willing to write?

Can the writer choose his own topic? Does the writer know the audience for whom he is writing?

Can the writer stay focused on the topic? Can he sustain his attention throughout the piece?

Can the writer collect materials and organize information to support the topic?

Does the writer have some knowledge of text structures for creating a text?

Can the writer select the appropriate mode for writing?

Revising

Is the writer willing to revise?

Does the writer reread the message several times for clarity?

Does the writer share the text with listeners to ensure that the meaning is clear to the audience?

Can the writer make good word choices for communicating the clearest message?

Does the writer use revising techniques as tools for clarifying and extending the meaning of the text?

Editing

Is the writer willing to edit?

Does the writer edit for spelling errors by circling words and making multiple attempts toward a correct spelling?

Does the writer edit for punctuation and grammar?

Does the writer edit for paragraph structure?

Can the writer use resources (spelling charts, dictionaries, editing checklists) to edit his work?

Publishing

Does the writer understand that publishing means error-free texts?

Can the writer plan and organize the final draft for publication?

Does the writer share the published work with an audience?

Figure 3.2 Exhibit of children's writing.

Organizing for Writers' Workshop

The block of time for writers' workshop in first- to third-grade classrooms varies from forty-five minutes to one hour. In the kindergarten classroom, we allow approximately thirty to forty minutes.

In kindergarten, the children participate in daily assisted writing experiences (e.g., shared writing, modeled writing, interactive writing); and, in the process, they acquire some knowledge about the printed word. Then, the teacher implements writers' workshop into the literacy block. Certainly, it is important to note that during the independent writing component, children will be at various stages in their writ-

ing development. Thus, some children will have more difficulty in sustaining their attention on the writing task, especially if their transcribing skills are limited. This implies that teachers will need to monitor their students' needs and adjust the writing format according-ly. With this in mind, here is a flexible structure that teachers can use to implement a writers' workshop in a kindergarten classroom.

Shared Writing Event

The teacher engages the children in an interactive writing experience, for instance, writing a story, a letter, or a poem. The interaction focuses on composing a message and transcribing the text. The teacher uses the writing context to help children acquire some critical skills for learning about print. This shared event lasts about ten to fifteen minutes.

Independent Writing

The children begin writing on a topic of their own choice. Most children use a spiral-bound notebook with unlined pages. Teachers like this format because the writing is kept together in one book, and they can study how children's writing has changed over time. Also, the children like the idea of looking through the notebook and seeing how they have grown as writers. Additionally, children might write on loose sheets of lined and unlined paper. This period of independent writing is generally fifteen to twenty minutes.

Conferences

As the children write, the teacher conducts individual conferences of about five minutes per child. He begins by asking the child to point to the words and read the story; he praises the child for the message; and finally, he directs the child's attention to accurate letter/sound relationships and words that the child has spelled correctly. Generally, the teacher can confer with about three students during independent writing time. In addition to individual conferences, the teacher circulates among the children and observes them as they write. (See Chapter 5 for an example of a kindergarten conference.)

Sharing

Students share their stories with their classmates. Most classrooms establish a designated spot in the room for the sharing event; for instance, an author's chair can become a special place where students share their written pieces with others. This component lasts about five to ten minutes. (However, it is important to note that students also share their writing at other times during the day.)

If first-graders have come from a kindergarten classroom where writing is a natural part of their day, they move easily into a first-grade writers' workshop. They have developed a habit of writing, and they've acquired some phonological and orthographic information for recording their text. The basic format for writers' workshop in first to third grades is the same.

Mini-Lesson

Mini-lessons are explicit and focused lessons that the teacher creates to demonstrate a particular skill or strategy. The demonstrations are planned according to the needs of the class as a whole. This means that the teacher must recognize that some children will need additional support beyond the mini-lessons, while a smaller group of children may already understand the skill being taught. (This is the compromise teachers must make anytime we teach to a whole class.) Yet, the mini-lesson plays an important role in writers' workshop because it provides the teacher with a daily context for teaching children critical skills and particular content for success in writing. During the lesson, the teacher carefully observes her students and makes mental notes of those who might need extra support during writing conferences and small-group assisted writing lessons. Mini-lessons are designed to be specific and brief, lasting on average about ten minutes.

Independent Writing

It is critical that young writers have a block of time to write independently. Here, they choose their own topics and apply their knowledge of the writing process to their work. Since their writing will be at different stages, it is important that children know how to use resources (editing checklists, writing charts, text guides, dictionaries, writing folders) to help themselves when the teacher is not available. The independent writing block should last for at least thirty minutes.

Conferences

During individual conferences, the teacher is able to tailor his guidance to the needs of the student. For instance, if a child is having trouble with locating misspelled works in his story, the teacher can support him in this area. Or if a child is experiencing difficulty with starting a new story, the teacher can show him how to create a topic list. The point here is that individual conferences enable teachers to personalize their support of children's writing.

Sharing of Published Work

It is important that students recognize the purpose of publishing their work for an audience. Teachers confer with students to ensure that they publish at least ten pieces a year. When a text is published, the student signs up for a sharing session. He reads his story to his classmates, and they comment on specific parts of the text that they enjoyed. (After a story is published, peers do not offer feedback for changes. Instead, this type of feedback should occur during peer conferences and before publication.) Generally, teachers schedule this event one or two times a week, with approximately ten minutes per session. Also, students might share their published work at other times during the day.

Learning to Manage the Writing Process

When students learn how to self-manage their writing environment, they have more time to spend on the actual tasks of writing. Thus, in writers' workshop, we allow time to teach children organizational skills for storing and using their writing materials. Then children become familiar with using specific writing tools, and they expect these resources to be helpful for guiding their own writing progress. Let's look at three writing tools that students use for organizing their work, collecting ideas, and reflecting on their performance.

Writing Portfolio

The portfolio is a special folder for storing a collection of the student's writing pieces over time. The teacher keeps a large container with hanging folders in an accessible place in the classroom, where the student can file his writing. On a regular basis, the student goes through his portfolio and evaluates some of his pieces. He makes decisions regarding the contents of the portfolio, such as choosing particular pieces to work on later, taking certain pieces home, or using an existing piece to develop a new idea. The writing portfolio is a valuable resource tool for the student, as it presents him with a personal storehouse of his writing accomplishments over time. Figure 3.3 shows a first-grade student reading through several writing pieces in his portfolio; he reflects on the quality of his work and considers which pieces he would like to keep in his folder.

Writer's Log

This is a small journal or composition book that the student uses to record feelings, thoughts, and ideas as they occur to her. The student car-

Figure 3.3 A student reflects on work from his writing portfolio.

ries the log around to write notes and capture impressions from her environment. The writer's log is an important tool, for it contains a wealth of ideas for developing or enhancing a piece of writing.

Writing Notebook

The writing notebook is a folder with pockets for storing the writing forms and current pieces of writing that the student is working on. Basically, it is a self-management tool that enables the student to store in one place all the forms and checklists that she might need for writing. Figure 3.4 illustrates how the writing notebook is organized.

We use a plastic spiral bound folder with eight pockets for inserting papers. This is a common folder that can be purchased at an office supply store. Notice that a plastic zippered pouch is included at the front of the notebook. This is an important accessory to the folder because it holds necessary writing tools (yellow highlighter, small pad of Post-it notes, red pen, thin blue marker, pencil). To add this piece to the writer's folder, we use a binding machine to punch holes in the pouch and then insert the pouch into the spiral binding.

Forms for Self-Regulated Writing

A critical feature of self-regulated writers is their ability to use resources as reflective tools for guiding and evaluating their performance on a particular task. In this section, we share several forms to be included in the student's

Figure 3.4 A writing notebook.

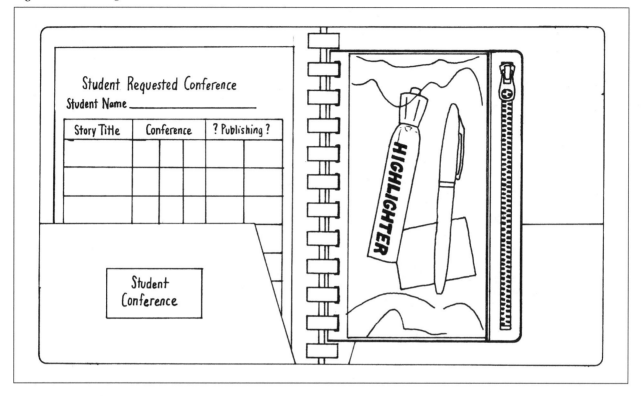

writing notebook, but keep in mind that no form is added to the notebook until students understand the purpose of the form. This means that teachers must introduce each form at a meaningful and relevant point in children's writing development. Meaningfulness occurs when students have the background knowledge and experiences to make sense of the task at hand. Relevance occurs when students can take the form and use it appropriately to help themselves on a particular task.

Before introducing a new form to students, we must ask, Do the students have the skills and knowledge to use the form for guiding and evaluating their own writing performance? If the answer is yes, then teachers can use simple guidelines to introduce a new writing form to their students. This is a basic format that we use in our classrooms.

- *Introduce the form in a focused mini-list.* Go over each step to ensure that the students understand the intention behind the specific prompts on the form. Apply the prompts to a writing sample: give a clear demonstration and use explicit language. The teacher might introduce only one prompt at a time. For instance, on the editing chart the prompt "Circle the words that do not look right" might take an entire mini-lesson. The point here is that teachers make good decisions about how much new information should be included in each mini-lesson. (See Chapter 4 for details on mini-lessons.)
- *Expect students to use the form as a self-help tool.* Show the children where the new form is kept in their writing notebook and explain where they can get additional

forms, if needed. Inform the children that you will count on them to bring their writing notebook to each conference and that they should use the appropriate form, prior to the conference, to guide and check on their writing.

- *Observe the children as they write, and expect that some children will need extra help in using the forms appropriately.* Because of the diversity of students' learning zones in a classroom, some students will need extra help in understanding the purpose of the writing form. This can occur during individual conferences or small-group mini-lessons. Look for opportunities to provide more personalized guidance and scaffolding for students who need extra help.
- *Use the form during conferences.* Begin each conference by asking the student to show you where he is in the writing process. If a writing form is appropriate for a particular conference, the teacher might refer to this form. (See Chapter 5 for details on conferences.)

Recall from Figure 3.4 that writing forms are stored in the student's writing notebook. Once again, it is important to emphasize that these forms are not included in the notebook until they have been introduced in mini-lessons. Thus, a writing notebook will look different at the beginning of the year than at the end of the year. Now let's look at some forms from the writing notebooks of first-grade students (Figure 3.5) that students use for monitoring, planning, revising, and reflecting on their writing.

Student-Scheduled Conferences On this form, the student documents his conference with the teacher, including the topic, date, and publishing information. Here, we can see that Nathan has requested a conference with his

Figure 3.5 Forms to assist self-regulated writing. Appendix D provides blank forms.

Student-Scheduled Conferences

Story Title	Plan	Draft	Revise	Edit	? Publishing ?	
My Pet Frog		✓ 11-20-99		✓ 12-5-99	(yes)	no
My Vacation	12-10-99			✓ 12-15-99	yes	(no)
Magnets	1-10-00	1-6-00		✓ 1-13-00	(yes)	no
Beekeepers	2-5-00			2-8-00	yes	no
Letter to my grandma	2-10-00	2-13-00		2-15-00 mailed	(yes)	no
The Big Catch				2-25-00	yes	(no)
The missing Shoe				3-1-00	yes	(no)
Gunner's toy			3-8-00		yes	(no)
My broken leg		3-16-00	3-16-00	3-18-00	(yes)	no
					yes	no
					yes	no
					Yes	no
					Yes	no

teacher on nine occasions. The topics indicate that he has written different types of texts and that he has published four pieces and mailed a letter. This form provides important information on the student's ability to self-regulate his need for assistance. For example, if a student is requesting too many conferences, he might be becoming too dependent on the teacher. On the other hand, if a student never requests a conference with the teacher, this might be a sign that the student is too comfortable with his work.

Topic List This form includes story ideas that the student has recorded as potential writing topics. When she cannot think of a story to

Figure 3.5 *(continued)*

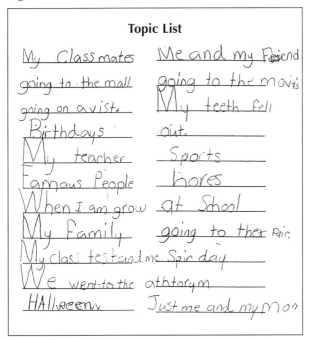

Figure 3.5 *(continued)*

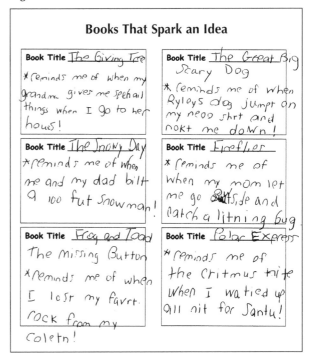

Figure 3.5 *(continued)*

write about, the student can use her topic list as a source of ideas. On Trovana's list, she has added topic ideas at different times—whenever an idea occurs to her.

Books That Spark an Idea This form is used to record ideas that develop from reading. For instance, when his teacher was reading the book *The Giving Tree* (Silverstein 1964), Nathan wrote, "[The book] reminds me of when my grandma gives me special things when I go to her house." Then, on another day, in writers' workshop, Nathan wrote a story about a special trip to his grandmother's farm.

Action Words This form is used to record action words that the writer might include in a story. The student understands that strong verbs are critical to a piece of writing, so when he thinks of a good action word, he records it on this list. As children become more competent writers, they begin to categorize these words into groups. For instance, Nathan has placed a bracket around several words that could be substituted for *said*. Also, the list is cumulative and includes words from both reading and writing experiences over the year.

Describing Words This form is used to record lists of describing words that the student might include in her writing. The list is first started in a mini-lesson, but later the student adds interesting words on her own. This list is cumulative and includes words from the student's reading and writing experiences over the year.

Writing Checklist This checklist is an important tool for monitoring and reflecting on the quality of a student's writing. The student uses the steps outlined on the checklist to reread, revise, and edit her piece. A check mark is

Figure 3.5 *(continued)*

Figure 3.5 *(continued)*

Writing Checklist

1. Read your story out loud to make sure it makes sense. _____✓_____

2. Add to your story or X out what you don't want. _____✓_____

3. Circle words that do not look right. _____✓_____

4. Use trial page to check spellings. _____✓_____

5. Look up the circled words. _____✓_____

6. Read your story out loud. Listen for where your voice stops. Add punctuation. _____✓_____

7. Check for capitalization at the beginning of your sentences. _____✓_____

Figure 3.5 *(continued)*

Describing Words

beautiful	flowery
pretty	curved
lovely	pearly
awesome	happy
small	long
sharp	hairy
slanted	~~bared~~
big	~~quiet~~ sleepy
large	grassy
little	stubby
gigantic	steep
enormous	bright
frightful	swirling
terrible	dark
color words	woolen
old	huge
new	great
cozy	fantastic

Figure 3.5 *(continued)*

Publishing a Book

Read your story and decide how to organize the sentences into a book.

Use a red pen to separate your story into pages. _____✓_____

How many pages will you need? Gather the number of pages for your book. 13

Rewrite story in your neatest writing. _____✓_____

Draw the pictures on each page to illustrate your story. _____✓_____

Write the title and author on the cover page. ✓ The Lost Dog

Write an author's page at the end of your book. ✓

Staple or bind your book. _____

Share your book. _____

placed next to the completed step, and the checklist is filed with the writing piece. When the student confers with the teacher, the writing checklist is used as a resource for final editing.

Publishing a Book This checklist guides students through the steps of organizing a writing piece for publication. It includes specifics, such as page layout, pictures, title, author's page, and binding considerations. After a writing piece has been edited, the student uses this form to prepare the piece for publication.

Spelling Trial Page This form is used for trying out different spellings for a word. In a draft, the student circles words that do not look right and records several of these words in the

first column on the spelling trial page. Then he tries another spelling in the second column. He compares the two choices and, if necessary, looks up the correct spelling in the dictionary. He uses the yellow marker to highlight the part within the word that was misspelled. This form provides a cumulative listing of spelling words that are categorized in his word study notebook (see Dorn and Soffos 2001a for more details).

Word Choices An extension of this list is a writing form that students use for evaluating and revising their word choices for a writing piece. They reread the text for the quality of their word choices; they use a yellow marker to highlight several words (nouns, verbs, adjec-

Figure 3.5 *(continued)*

Spelling Trial Page		
First Try	**Second Try**	**Correct**
streat	Street ✓	Street
lookt	lookte	looked
plae	play ✓	play
ucros	ucross	across
pane	pain ✓	pain
hite	night ✓	night
noo	now	new
far ✓	far ✓	far
cart	cart	cart
cool	cool (zoo) ✓	cool
crie	crie	cry
faster	faster ✓	faster
looking ✓		looking
owr	our ✓	our
howse	house ✓	house
wen	when ✓	when
pleaz	pleas	please

Figure 3.5 *(continued)*

Word Choices		
My word	**Other words**	**Final choice**
bumpy	rocky	rocky
burst	explode ✓	explode
bright	shiny sparkling	sparkling
chubby	plump ✓	plump
liquid	watery	liquid
promise	swear	promise
quiet	peaceful	peaceful
flood	overflow	flood
giant	enormous	enormous
flee	escape	flee
house	shelter	shelter
throw	toss	toss
lid	cover	lid
scrub	wipe	scrub
mystery	secret ✓	secret
puddle	pool	puddle
dash	dart	dart

tives); they record these words on their word choice list. Then they think of other words that might be substituted. This form provides a cumulative listing of word choices with similar meanings.

Text Guides and Checklists

In addition to these forms, a writing notebook will include text guides and checklists for composing in different modes. The teacher assists the children in developing these guides. The text guides are directly linked to reading activities; for instance, after reading several types of informational texts, the teacher and students might develop a text guide for this style of writing. Then, in an assisted writing lesson or a group mini-lesson, the teacher demonstrates how to use the text guide during writing. A complementary form to the text guide is the writing checklist. In Chapter 2, we presented two examples of tall tales written by third-grade students who used a text guide and a writing checklist to help themselves. These two sources are designed to scaffold writers to organize their writing according to characteristics of a particular mode of writing, and to self-reflect on the quality of their writing in relation to these specific text criteria. The goal of these guides is that students will internalize the characteristics for particular texts; then these guides will not be needed to support the writing process. Here are three examples of text guides and the writing checklists that match them.

Informational Text Guide and Checklist A text guide and checklist for informational texts are shown in Figure 3.6. The text guide is designed to support writers in organizing factual information for a particular audience. Students need to understand that informational texts must be accurate and up-to-date. Thus,

Figure 3.6 Text guide and checklist for informational writing. Appendix E provides blank forms.

Text Guide for Writing Informational Texts

1. Choose your topic. _BeeKeepers_

2. Use up-to-date and accurate resources to learn about your topic. _BeeKeepers_ _____

3. Use notes or diagrams to organize your information. ① hives ② how bees make honey ③ extractors _____

4. Use a good opening sentence to introduce your topic. _BeeKeepers have hives and they are colored._

Figure 3.6 (continued)

Checklist for Informational Texts

1. Did you use up-to-date and accurate resources to learn about your topic? ___✓___

2. Did you use notes or diagrams to organize your information? ___✓___

3. Did you use a good opening sentence to introduce your topic? ___✓___

4. Did you organize your information in an orderly format? ___✓___

5. Did you include accurate facts? ___✓___

6. Did you add details to explain your topic in clear language? ___✓___

7. Did you use a closing statement? ___✓___

students learn how to gather facts on a specific topic and incorporate this information into their writing. The checklist provides students with an additional resource for evaluating the quality of their writing according to the criteria for this type of text. Figure 3.7 shows Riley's first draft of his report on beekeepers, which indicates that he understands the criteria for writing informational texts. In his piece, he includes accurate information, organizes details in an orderly format, and uses clear language to explain his topic.

Mystery Checklist This checklist states the essential features of a mystery, including the problem (the mystery), the clues, and the steps involved in solving the mystery. While reading, students will have acquired an understanding of the characteristics of mysteries. At that time, the teacher coaches them to articulate the critical features of this genre. They use this checklist to help themselves compose their own mystery stories. After writing the story, students use the mystery checklist (Figure 3.8) to assess the quality of their compositions according to the criteria for this genre. Let's see how Heather, a first-grade writer, has incorporated the essential features of a mystery into her own written production. This is the first mystery that she has written, yet she shows evidence that she understands how mysteries are organized. For instance, she includes a

Figure 3.7 Riley's report on beekeepers (first grade).

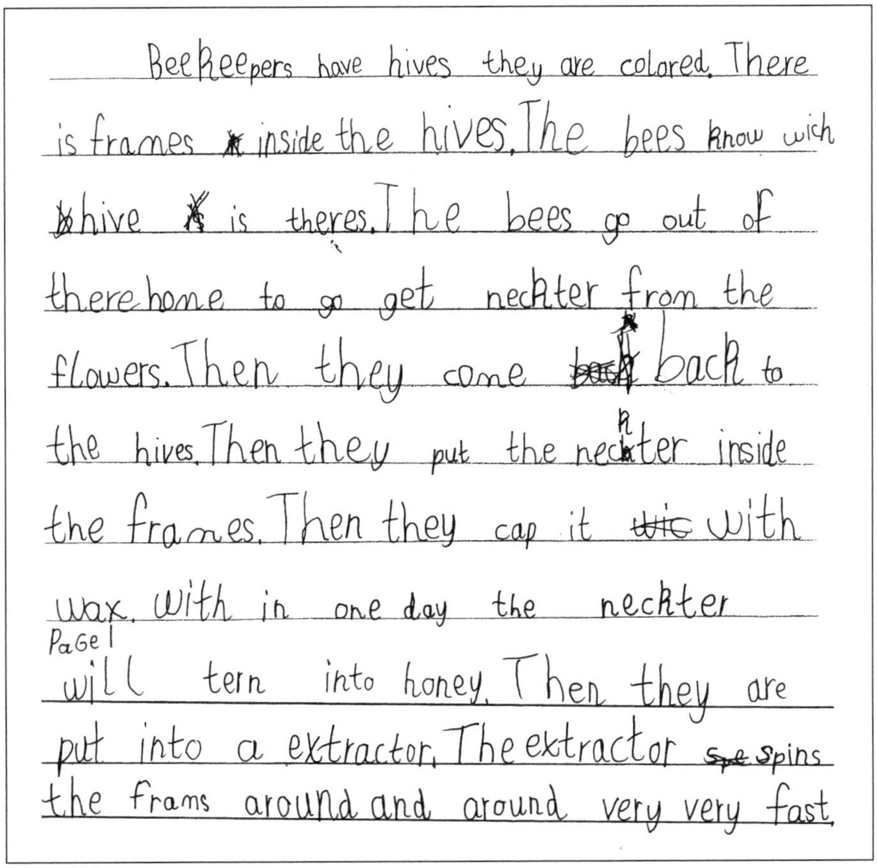

Beekeepers have hives they are colored. There is frames inside the hives. The bees know wich hive is theres. The bees go out of there home to go get nechter from the flowers. Then they come back to the hives. Then they put the nechter inside the frames. Then they cap it with wax. With in one day the nechter will tern into honey. Then they are put into a extractor. The ektractor spins the frams around and around very very fast.

Page 1

Figure 3.8 Checklist for mystery. Appendix F provides a blank form.

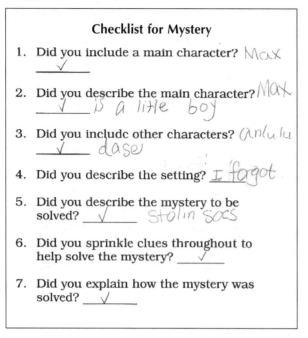

Checklist for Mystery

1. Did you include a main character? Max ✓

2. Did you describe the main character? Max ✓ is a little boy

3. Did you include other characters? anlulu ✓ dase

4. Did you describe the setting? I forgot.

5. Did you describe the mystery to be solved? ✓ Stolin socs

6. Did you sprinkle clues throughout to help solve the mystery? ✓

7. Did you explain how the mystery was solved? ✓

main character and other characters who assist in solving the mystery, and she builds a suspenseful pattern through repeating actions as the characters strive to find the missing socks. Heather sprinkles two clues into her story, which lead to the final resolution and the solving of the mystery. During a writing conference, the teacher can guide Heather to use the checklist to evaluate her mystery according to the criteria.

The Mystery of the Stolen Socks

There was a little boy. His name is Max. He lost a pair of socks. They are my only socks! "I will have to investigate," he said. "But first I have to go to school." Then when Max got home from school, he began to investigate! "Where are my socks?" Maybe they're under the couch. They are not here. Then one of Max's friends came over. Her name is Angela. She said, "Hi Max." "Hi Angela," said Max. "I'm glad you came! They are my favorite socks!" Then another one

of his friends came over. Her name is Daisy! "Hi Max," said Daisy! "Hi, Daisy!" said Max. "I'm glad you can come!" Then Daisy found a clue. "It is a dog." "A dog!" Max said. "Yes! A dog must have chewed your sock," said Daisy. "Good grief!" said Max. Then another one of Max's friends came over. Her name is Lindsey.

"I'm glad you came," said Max. "What are you doing?" said Lindsey. "We are looking for something." "I will help," said Lindsey. "What are we looking for?" "We are looking for my socks," said Max. "I hope we find them!" said Lindsey. Then Lindsey found a clue. It is a string. "What good does a string do for us?" said Max. "Max someone must have torn your sock," said Daisy. "Hey," shouted Max. "I found a piece of my sock!" "Great!" said Daisy. "Now all we have to do is find the rest of your sock," said Daisy. "Ho, yes! I found my socks!" "Where were they?" said Daisy. "They were under my dresser," said Max.

Written Retelling Guide This retelling guide (Figure 3.9) is designed to scaffold students in composing a written retelling. During guided reading and read-aloud events, teachers coach students to attend to how stories are organized, for instance, the setting, the characters, the problem, the sequence of events, and the resolution. Also, teachers prompt students to think about beginning, middle, and ending components of a story. These oral language sessions around stories provide children with experiences for composing well-organized written retellings. Also, the guide serves the writer as an assessment tool for evaluating his retelling performance. In the following retelling, Alexis shows her understanding for a composition that meets the criteria for this mode.

The Wilde Street Club wanted a dog. So they went to the pound to get one. But when they got there, they could not find the one that they

Figure 3.9 Guide for written retelling. Appendix G provides a blank form.

Written Retelling

1. Write a good lead that grabs the attention of the reader. ___✓___

2. Write what happened first.___✓___

3. Write what happened next. ___✓___

4. Write what happened last. ___✓___

5. Include interesting details to describe the events. ___✓___

6. Use an appropriate ending. _____

7. React to the story in a personal way.

___ ___

Closing Thoughts

In this chapter, we have shared the practical side of writers' workshop, including specific details for implementing this component into a balanced literacy program. A major theme has been the need to create opportunities for young writers to develop independence. This is accomplished through predictable environments and writing tools that promote self-regulated writers. In Chapter 4, we continue this theme by discussing how teachers design clear and explicit mini-lessons. In all cases, the goal is to enable young writers to develop the skills and strategies they need to advance their writing to higher levels.

wanted. Some they could not tell heads from tails, some ate too much, some were too small. All the dogs just did not fit perfect for them. They saw a dog that was perfect but it had a piece of paper in its mouth. The dog had a collar on it. The dog's name was Molly. Molly wanted the Wilde Street Club to come with her. So the Wilde Street Club went with Molly. Molly led them to Mr. Lee, Molly's owner. Mr. Lee was hurt! Kerry called 911, the ambulance. The ambulance took Mr. Lee to the hospital. The Wilde Street Club took care of Molly. Molly liked the Wilde Street Club. Mr. Lee was better on Sunday, and he was back. The Wilde Street Club told Mr. Lee they could not find Molly. Mr. Lee said it was okay, Molly can take care of herself. Mr. Lee's son found Molly. Molly had puppies! Mr. Lee said they could have one when they were eight years old!

Designing Productive Mini-Lessons

In scaffolding young writers, teachers design instructional opportunities that include clear demonstrations, explicit teaching, guided assistance, and independent practice. Mini-lessons provide an ideal context for this type of teaching. Assessment informs instruction, and vice versa. Therefore, the success of mini-lessons is grounded in the teacher's knowledge of the writing process as it relates to students' writing development (see Figure 4.1). In designing mini-lessons, here are some questions that teachers might ask:

What do the students already know? Do they have the skills and background to interpret the mini-lesson? Is the lesson geared for the majority of the class? Does it provide a learning opportunity for all students, regardless of learning level?

What do the students need to know? What is the clearest and easiest way to demonstrate this information? What about students who have further to go in achieving the goal? How can these students be supported?

The goal of mini-lessons is that students will be able to accomplish a particular task with assistance from the teacher. The teacher closely observes the group, makes mental notes of students who will need extra help, and plans for ways to scaffold these students in small groups or individual conferences.

How can teachers design productive mini-lessons that lead to independence? What is the format for conducting mini-lessons? How can teachers incorporate skills into mini-lessons? What about the craft of writing? These are just a few of the questions that guide our discussion of mini-lessons for scaffolding young writers.

Planning for Mini-Lessons

An important characteristic of a well-designed mini-lesson is the explicit and focused nature of the lesson. Teachers use them as opportunities to advance children's learning to a higher level. If the lesson is too long, the teacher might be focusing on too many items, and the goal of instruction becomes unclear. The ultimate goal is that the students will understand

Figure 4.1 The interrelations between teaching writing and learning about writing.

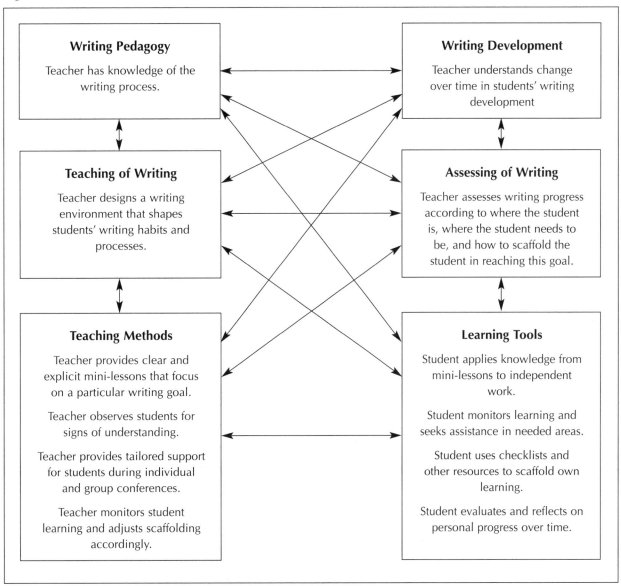

the intention of the lesson and thus be able to apply this knowledge at some level to independent writing.

Generally, the mini-lesson is divided into two distinct areas. First, the teacher demonstrates a specific writing skill or strategy. Next, if appropriate, the teacher coaches the students to apply this knowledge to a piece of writing from their writing notebooks. When students apply the new learning to their own work, the lesson becomes meaningful. However, the teacher understands that some students will need additional scaffolding when they begin their independent writing; writing conferences provide students with individualized support.

Basically, mini-lessons can be categorized under four broad areas: organization, strategies, skills, and author's craft. We've included some examples of mini-lessons that might fall under each category. Teachers can build on this list by including specific skills that might be important for their own primary-grade students.

Types of Mini-Lessons

Organization (What to Do): Procedural Knowledge for Implementing Specific Rules or Guidelines

- Rules and guidelines for writers' workshop
- How to set up a writing notebook (see example lesson)
- How to self-manage your writing environment
- How to use a writing portfolio
- How to use a writer's log
- How to locate materials (forms, portfolios) and resources
- How to use writing checklists and forms (see example lesson)
- How to help yourself when nobody is available to help you
- How to prepare for a teacher-scheduled conference
- How and when to request an additional conference
- How to conduct a peer conference (rules and guidelines)
- How to respond to peers when they share their published writing

Strategies (How to Do): Conceptual Knowledge for Thinking Processes

- How to revise your message for clarity of meaning
- How to expand the message
- How to stick to a topic (see example lesson)
- How to eliminate redundant and unnecessary information
- How to edit for spelling errors and use resources to self-correct (see example lesson)

- How to reread your writing from a reader's perspective
- How to rearrange your sentences or paragraphs for greater cohesion
- How to organize your text for a public audience (layout, pictures)
- How to write in different modes
- How to organize information for writing
- How to self-evaluate writing according to standards and good models
- How to compare writing performance over time

Skills (Specific What to Do): Knowledge of Grammar and Punctuation Rules

- How to use capitalization for beginning of sentence (see example lesson)
- How to use closing punctuation appropriately (see example lesson)
- How to use commas for words in a series
- How to use subject and verb agreement
- How to use pronouns correctly
- How to use capitalization for proper nouns
- How to organize paragraphs

Author's Craft (How to Write for an Audience): Creative Knowledge

- How to create good lead sentences or paragraphs (see example lesson)
- How to use figurative language (see example lesson)
- How to develop rich descriptions of characters
- How to attend to small details (see example lesson)
- How to create descriptive settings
- How to choose good words for communicating the best message
- How to create "mind pictures"
- How to use strong action verbs (see example lesson)
- How to create catchy endings

In the next section, we present examples of mini-lessons from each of these categories. First, we provide a detailed description of a teaching interaction; then we share sample pages from a teacher's mini-lesson notebook. In working with teachers, we've created a common format (introduce, discuss, apply) that provides them with a scaffold for developing their own lessons. We encourage you to use this simple framework to create productive mini-lessons to meet the needs of your own students.

Mini-Lessons on Organization

The success of writers' workshop is grounded in a well-organized program where students understand particular routines and procedures. Too often, we have observed in classrooms that the effectiveness of writers' workshop is diluted because the students do not understand the rules and guidelines for participating in the workshop. These include where their materials are located, how to use their notebooks, and how to help themselves when the teacher is unavailable. These behaviors are all associated with self-regulation, that is, the students' ability to self-manage and self-direct their own learning. In mini-lessons, teachers instruct students in organizational routines that promote productive writing experiences. Let's take a closer look at one classroom example of a mini-lesson from this category. At the end of the lesson, we've included an example from a first-grade teacher's notebook that focuses on the organizational aspects of writers' workshop.

How to Set Up a Writing Notebook

At an appropriate time in the school year, Carla introduces the writing notebook to first-graders. Prior to the lesson, she has prepared writing notebooks for all students. Today, she uses one example to direct the children's attention to two sections on the inside of the notebook: the zipper bag and the draft section. Here, it is important to note that the teacher does not introduce all sections at one time but rather at meaningful and relevant points in the students' writing program. The following transcript illustrates the explicit nature of the introduction to the writing notebook.

Teacher: Boys and girls, being organized during writers' workshop is very important. Having a special place to keep your materials and pieces of writing that you are working on is critical. So with that in mind, I have put together for each of you a writing folder. On the front of the writing notebook is your name, and when you open it, your zipper pouch is right on the inside. It holds your pencil and your marker that you will need when you write. In the back of your notebook is a section called the draft section. A draft means a piece of writing that you are still working on. You are just getting your ideas down on paper.

Next, Carla passes out the students' writing notebooks and guides them to locate the draft section. She hands them a piece of writing that they are currently working on, and the children insert it into the draft section. Then she prompts them to return to the front of the notebook where the zipper pouch is located. She encourages the students to explain why the zipper pouch is an important organizational tool to include in the writing notebook. Ricky responds, "It holds our pencils and markers." As the mini-lesson comes to a close, Carla says, "Now that you have all your drafts in your draft section, and marker and pencil in your zipper pouch, go back to your tables and begin writing. I'll check on you later."

How to Use Writing Checklists and Forms

Type of mini-lesson	Organization/Using topic list form
Materials	Transparency of Topic List form Topic List form for each student Student writing notebooks
Introduce the lesson	Tell the students that sometimes a writer has a difficult time thinking of a topic to write about. At other times, a writer has too many ideas to write about in a particular piece. Introduce the Topic List form as a resource for storing good ideas that can be developed at a later time.
Discuss the process	Model a think-aloud process for developing a topic list. Use a transparency of the Topic List form to record your ideas. Show the students where you will store your topic list in your writing notebook.
Apply the process	Engage the students in discussing some topics or ideas they would like to write about. Tell them to record the ideas on their Topic List form. Ask if students are ready to begin a new piece of writing. Encourage these students to use their topic list as a resource for developing a new topic for writing.

Mini-Lessons on Strategies

During mini-lessons, teachers use clear and memorable examples that provide students with models for learning how to problem-solve during writing. Teachers strive to create learning opportunities that promote self-regulated writers. Therefore, strategy lessons are an essential part of writers' workshop. Here, teachers focus on a specific writing strategy, for instance, how to revise or edit a piece of writing. In this section, we discuss how Teresa guides her first-graders to apply editing strategies to their writing; then we share an example of sticking to a topic from Lance's notebook of mini-lessons.

How to Edit for Spelling Errors and Use Resources to Self-Correct

By mid-year, Teresa's first-grade students have learned how to self-monitor their spellings for words that do not look right. Today, the focus of the mini-lesson is to coach students in using their trial page and dictionary as self-help resources. Teresa places Patrick's story on the overhead projector and uses it to demonstrate this strategy. "Patrick, what do you need to do now?" Patrick responds, "Circle the words that do not look right." Patrick rereads his story, identifies and circles misspelled words. Then Teresa says, "I think you can figure out the correct spellings of these words before using the dictionary." She places a transparency of the trial page on the overhead projector and coaches Patrick to copy the first circled word from his story in the first column on the trial page. Then Patrick identifies the part of the word he is unsure of and uses a yellow marker to highlight the tricky part. Teresa asks, "Can you think of another way to write the word that would make it look right?" Patrick makes another attempt in the second column. Then Teresa models for Patrick and the other students how to use the dictionary to check on the correct spelling. Patrick writes the word accurately under the correct column; then Teresa coaches the students to apply the process to two new examples. As the lesson comes to a close, she reminds Patrick, "Now that you know how to use your trial page and dictionary, you can work on other words that you've circled." In Figures 4.2a and 4.2b, we can see how Patrick has applied the knowledge gained from the mini-lesson to his unassisted work. Later, when he meets with his teacher for a conference, he will bring his spelling trial page with him for a final spelling check.

Figure 4.2a Patrick's draft with words that don't look right circled (first grade).

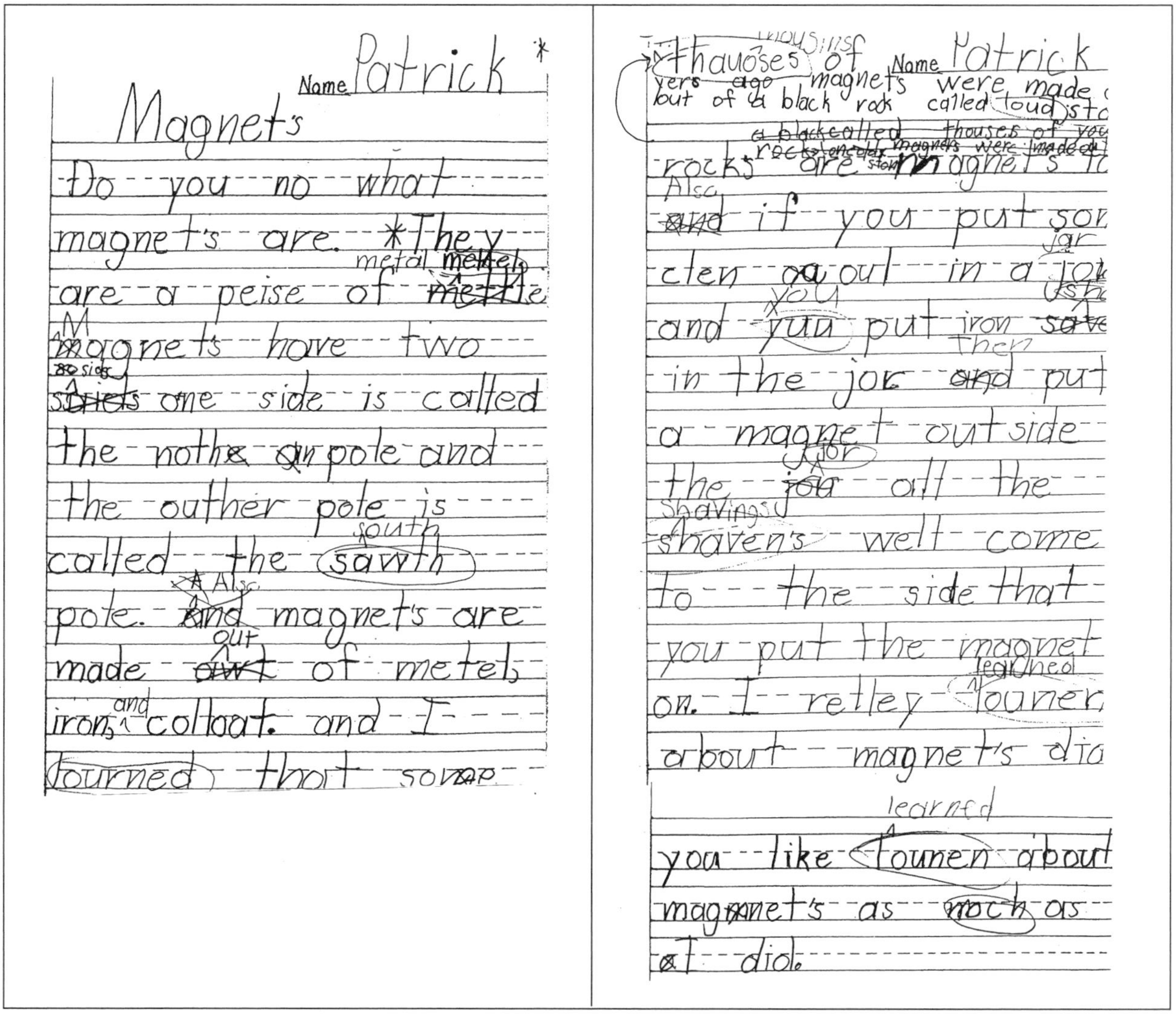

Figure 4.2b Patrick's spelling trial page.

First Try	Second Try	Correct
peise	pise	piece
mettle	mettel	metal
Saids	side ✓	side
Sawth	South	South
Owt	out ✓	out
lourned	learned	learned
jor	jor	jar
shaven's	shavings	shavings
moch	much ✓	much

How to Stick to a Topic

Type of mini-lesson	Strategy/Stick to the topic
Materials	*The Very Hungry Caterpillar* Student writing notebooks
Introduce the lesson	Hold up the book, *The Very Hungry Caterpillar* by Eric Carle. Ask the students to predict what they think the book will be about. Elicit responses and ask why no one predicted the story would be about space. Tell the students that when we read this story, we expect it to be about a hungry caterpillar. Explain that sticking to the topic is important when writing so that the reader will not be confused. Invite them to listen to the story and see if Eric Carle sticks to his topic throughout the book.
Discuss the process	Ask the students if their predictions were correct. Did the author stick to the topic, or did he wander off and start writing about space?
Apply the process	Ask the students to open their writing notebooks and take out the drafts they are working on. Ask them to reread what they have written so far. Are they sticking to their topic? If they find a place where they have not, ask them to put their finger on that place. Then have one or two students share their pieces and invite other students to react. Then remind the students that before they continue to write they need to mark out the part that is not needed for that piece of writing.

Mini-Lessons on Skills

The skills for mini-lessons are based on district and state standards for specific areas of competence at each grade level. Teachers use mini-lessons as opportunities to teach skills in meaningful and relevant contexts. In the next example, Sarah guides her second-graders to edit for closing punctuation. Then, we provide an example of capitalization from Donnie's notebook of mini-lessons.

How to Use Closing Punctuation

Sarah gathers her group of students around the overhead projector. She has selected Brittanie's writing as a good model for guiding the students to attend to the role of punctuation for enhancing meaning. Sarah invites Brittanie to read her story to the class. "As you read," she says, "listen to where your voice stops. We will help you with adding the punctuation in the correct places." As Brittanie reads her story, the students listen and offer feedback. One student comments, "You need to put an exclamation mark after 'I heard something in the bushes.'" Brittanie reads this line with expression and agrees. Figure 4.3 shows her corrected draft. The goal of the mini-lesson is accomplished, and the students choose a piece of their own writing to edit for punctuation.

Figure 4.3 Brittanie's draft with punctuation (second grade).

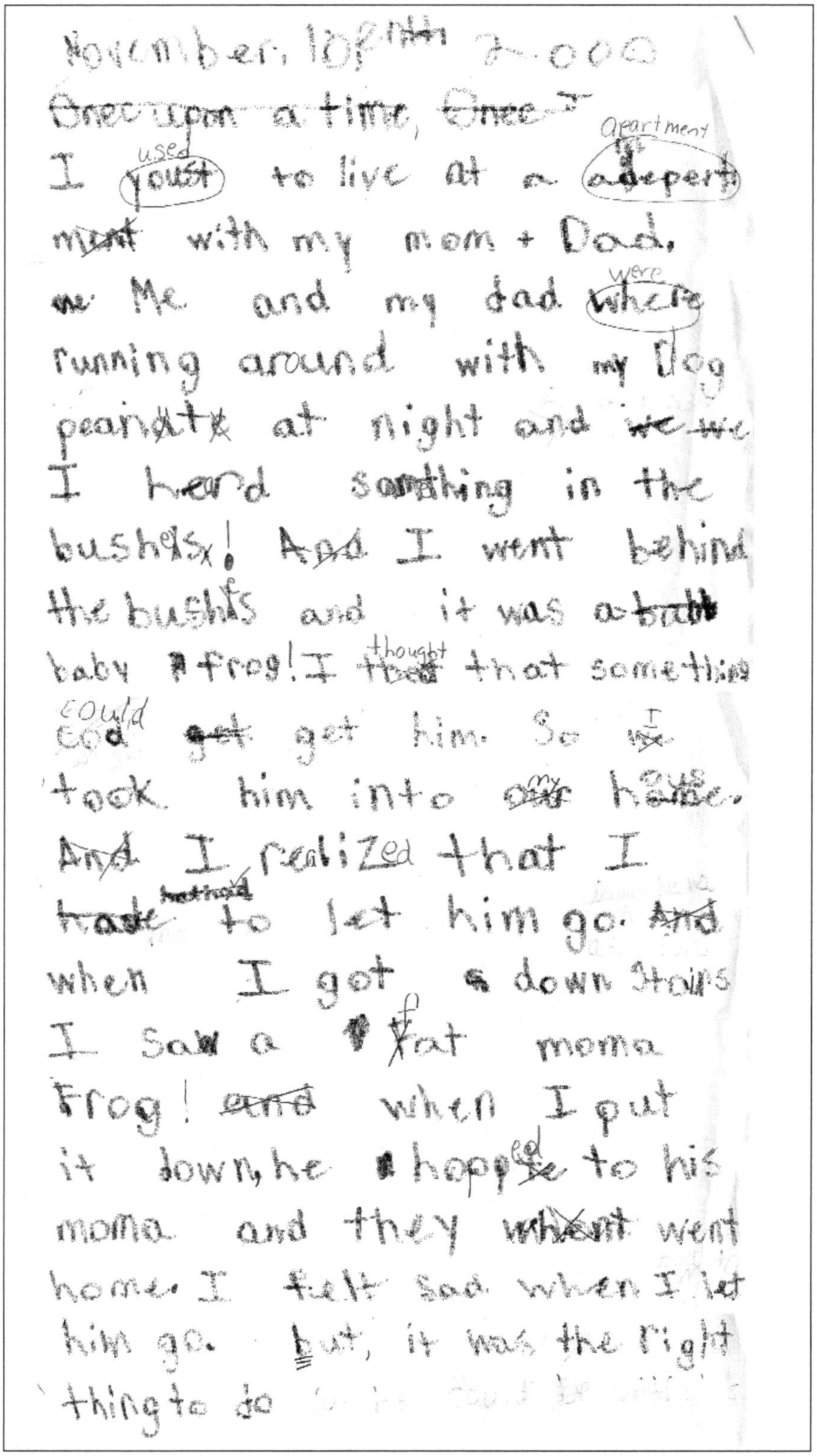

November, 10th 2,000
Once upon a time, once
I youst to live at a apartment
ment with my mom + Dad,
we Me and my dad where
running around with my dog
peanute at night and we we
I heard something in the
bushes! And I went behind
the bushes and it was a bad
baby a frog! I thought that something
could cod get get him. So I I
took him into our my house.
And I realized that I
have to let him go. And
when I got a down stairs
I saw a f fat moma
Frog! and when I put
it down, he a hopped to his
moma and they whent went
home. I felt sad when I let
him go. but, it was the right
thing to do

How to Use Beginning Capitalization

Type of mini-lesson	Skills/Using beginning capitalization
Materials	Transparency of student's writing that has already been edited for punctuation and is now ready for beginning capitalization. Student writing notebooks
Introduce the lesson	Explain to the students that they will reread a piece of writing that has already been edited for punctuation. Tell them that they will use this piece of writing to learn about beginning capitalization.
Discuss the process	Reread the writing piece. Guide the students to locate the ending punctuation. Show them how to edit for capitalization by drawing three lines under the first letter of the word that needs to be capitalized. Explain to the students that these marks will remind them to capitalize these words in their final draft.
Apply the process	Ask the students to take out a piece of writing from the draft section of their writing notebook. Tell them to reread the first sentence in their piece. Have them highlight the ending punctuation and then draw three editing lines under the first letter of the word that needs to be capitalized. Tell them that if they choose to publish this piece, they will need to continue with the editing process.

Mini-Lessons on Author's Craft

Teachers design mini-lessons that guide children to notice how writers write, including language, text conventions, and special techniques for communicating meanings to particular audiences. They use literature as a tool for directing children's attention to the craft of writing. For instance, teachers might read the beginning sections from two or three books and coach children to describe how the writer has captured the reader's attention with good lead sentences or paragraphs. Or, as illustrated in the first example, the teacher might use a section of student writing for the same purpose. As students gain more experiences with good writing, they acquire important models for comparing with their own work. They start to attend to the details of writing, for example, how words are used to develop characters and settings. Fletcher and Portalupi (1998) explain how the smallest details can provide the richest impressions and encourage teachers to design mini-lessons that teach this craft. In the second example, Linda guides her third-graders to focus on small images that create rich impressions in a reader's mind. The two final examples illustrate how teachers have designed mini-lessons that focus on figurative language and action words.

How to Develop a Good Lead

In this example of a third-grade writer, Justin is working on the craft of developing good lead sentences. Carla realizes that several students are ready to focus on this area in their own writing, so she designs a small-group mini-lesson around this topic. First, she reviews the importance of good lead sentences or sections that grab the reader's attention. Then she says, "Justin has agreed to let us use his story for discussing lead sentences." She places a transparency of Justin's writing on the overhead screen, invites him to read the story, and guides the students to focus their attention on the opening sentences. As Justin reads his sentences ("Don't do drugs. My cousin Jarred got hooked on drugs when he was in the ninth grade"), Carla records them on the chart tablet. Justin reflects, "I don't like the way that starts." Carla places a check mark next to the sentences, and Ashley suggests they try a lead that begins with a question. The group composes a second opening: "Have you seen anyone on drugs? My cousin Jarred got hooked on drugs when he was in the ninth grade." Then Carla asks, "Justin, how did your cousin describe his experience with drugs?" Justin comments, "He told me it was like being in a dark hole and he couldn't get out." Ashley exclaims, "Put that at the beginning! It makes you want to know more about what happened to Jarred." Carla guides the students to compare the three openings, and Justin decides on the final lead.

> When you do drugs your life is dark. It's like being in a cave and you can't get out. My older cousin Jarred got hooked on drugs when he was in the ninth grade. It was awful for our whole family. We all cried a lot. It all started when he moved to a new city and started hanging around with a bunch of bad kids that spent all their time doing drugs. They would all go out and the bad guys would say to Jarred, "Don't be a freak, pretty boy." So he let them get the best of him and he did drugs with them. He really didn't want to but he wanted to be a part of a group. Time went on and Jarred and his friends continued the bad stuff. Jarred flunked out of school, didn't get along with his family and acted really sad all the time. My aunt and uncle took him to a hospital and he had to stay there for a long time and get treatment for his problem. My family and I went to see Jarred and I'll never forget him saying to me, "Don't

do drugs. When I did them I felt like I was lost in a dark cave and couldn't get out. The drugs just take hold of your life and twist it the wrong way." He finally got well and now he helps other people who are on drugs. I am glad that I experienced that because I will never let that happen to me. Life is too valuable to spend it like that. Some kids never get off drugs and they miss all the fun things in life.

As the mini-lesson comes to a close, Carla says, "Go back to your desk and look in your folder for a writing piece that you would like to revise for a better lead sentence."

How to Attend to Small Details

In this example, Linda guides her third-grade students to consider ways that writers use words to create mind pictures for their readers. She explains, "Sometimes the smallest details in our writing can provide the reader with the most vivid images." She describes how writers use their eyes, ears, and touch to discover interesting details about their world. "These small details," she explains "can bring life into a piece of writing. As writers, we need to keep a writer's log with us at all times to record these small images." She pulls out her own writer's log and turns to a blank page. "I'm interested in writing a story about my cat, and I need to find the right words to describe her—the way she moves and feels, the way she sounds and smells." As she thinks aloud, Linda records words in her writer's log. She explains that she will continue to add new words as images of her cat come to mind. She encourages the students to use their writer's log for recording small details and images. Following this mini-lesson, Megan begins to record words in her writer's log to describe the silence of her world. Then she uses these words to create a poem:

The Sounds of Silence
When the whole class is silent
I hear many things.
Like the buzzing of the light
And the children on the swings.
I hear the wind as its limbs
Brush the window pane
And the gentle pitter patter
Of the fresh spring rain.

When my room is silent
I hear the mockingbird
Pecking its beak against the tree.
I can hear the pretty song
Of a redbird singing to me.

How to Use Figurative Language

Type of mini-lesson	Author's craft/Using figurative language
Materials	*The Listening Walk* by Paul Showers Transparency of a page from book Student writing notebooks
Introduce the lesson	Explain to the students that authors use onomatopoeia or noise words to make their writing better and to help create for the reader what someone or something sounds like. As you read the story, tell them to listen for the sound words and see if the words help them to hear all the sounds the author heard on his walk.
Discuss the process	Show a page from the text on the overhead. Ask the children to identify some onomatopoeia words and discuss how they help the reader to hear the sounds even though the reader isn't there. Write these words on chart paper under the title "Onomatopoeia (Noise Words)." Display in the room for children to use as a resource. Also put a label on the front cover of the book "Onomatopoeia (Noise Words)" so the children can use the book as a resource, too.
Apply the process	Ask the children to open their writing notebooks and take out their drafts. Ask them to reread a piece of writing and locate a place they may want to add a noise word to help the reader hear the way someone or something sounded. Ask a few students to share with the group. Remind the students that as they write, they might want to use some onomatopoeia or noise words in their writing.

How to Use Strong Action Words

Type of mini-lesson	Author's craft/Using strong action words
Materials	*Big Al* by Andrew Clemens Transparency of a page from book Transparency of Action Words form Student writing notebooks
Introduce the lesson	Tell the students that today they will revisit one of their favorite stories, *Big Al* by Andrew Clemens. Read a page from the transparency and ask the students to listen for how the author used strong action words to describe the action.
Discuss the process	Elicit responses from the students and guide them to tell you how the words described the actions. Underline the action words from the transparency page. Record the action words on the transparency of Action Words form.
Apply the process	Tell the students to record the words from the transparency on their Action Words form. Ask the students to open their writing notebooks and take out their current drafts. Ask them to reread their drafts and locate a place where they could substitute a stronger action word for the word in their text. Remind them that they could use the Action Words form.

Closing Thoughts

In this chapter, we have discussed the importance of well-designed mini-lessons for scaffolding young writers. An important theme has been the importance of clear and explicit teaching with a goal of promoting independence in writing. The mini-lesson provides young writers with a meaningful and relevant context for learning about the skills, strategies, and crafts of writing. In Chapter 5, we continue the discussion by exploring ways that teachers can support writers through individual and group conferences.

Writing Conferences

Throughout this book, we have emphasized the role of adults in scaffolding young writers. Teachers must be able to recognize the signs that students are becoming better at writing. With this in mind, teachers design instructional opportunities that are based on what writers know and what they need to know. Earlier, we discussed how mini-lessons provide focused opportunities to acquire new understandings about the writing process. Yet, we recognize the limitations of whole-group teaching: instruction that is just right for some students can be too easy or hard for others. Teachers accept this diversity as a condition of teaching and arrange for personalized opportunities to meet the needs of all students.

The writing conference is the heart of teaching the writing process. When teachers confer with children, they provide them with individualized guidance within their zone of proximal development. Graves (1994) states that "a rough profile of a good conference shows the child speaking about 80 percent of the time, the teacher 20 percent" (61). The very act of talking about writing involves both cognitive and social processes. During conferences

with a knowledgeable and responsive teacher, young writers learn how to formulate their thoughts into coherent and comprehensible messages.

The success of a writing conference is based on two types of knowledge: the teacher's knowledge of the writer and the teacher's knowledge of the process. This means that a teacher will respond differently to an early writer than to a fluent writer. The teacher's level of scaffolding will be gauged by the writer's ability to accomplish the task. In this chapter, we will look at how teachers use writing conferences to scaffold young writers at their cutting edge of development. First, we look at five types of writing conferences; then we share some examples from writers' workshop classrooms. (See Dorn and Soffos 2001a for video examples.)

Types of Writing Conferences

During writers' workshop, students can benefit from different types of writing conferences. The teacher makes decisions about the most productive conference for each student. All conferences share a common characteristic: they are brief, focused, and designed to actively engage the student in self-reflective learning.

Teacher-Scheduled Conferences

The teacher conducts an individual student conference for three to five minutes per day with at least five children. His goal is to meet with all the students in his class at least once a week. Also, this schedule ensures that the teacher will observe children at different points in the writing process (Figure 5.1). The teacher designates a special place in the room for these conferences.

Student-Scheduled Conferences

The student requests a conference if he feels a need for immediate help. If so, he records his name and the reason for the conference on a Request for Conference chart that is displayed in the room. When he confers with the teacher, he records notes on his personal conference form, which he keeps inside his writing notebook (see Figure 3.5). However, it is important to emphasize that students are encouraged to work on other writing projects prior to requesting a teacher conference. The goal is to promote self-regulated writers who understand that they can work on multiple pieces of writing at the same time. Too many requests for

Figure 5.1 Form for teacher-scheduled conferences. Appendix H provides a blank form.

Teacher-Scheduled Conferences

Student	Plan	Draft	Revise	Edit	Final	Teacher Notes
Cody				✓		Rereading and listening to where voice stops (A lot of scaffolding)
Kaylee			✓			Rereading - to help you think about what you need to say next (order)
Phillip					✓	Using publishing checklist - using red pen to separate pages.
Ceira		✓				How to record - saying words slowly and using ABC chart to help.
Sara			✓			Rereading story and deleting unnecessary information.

conferences might indicate that a student is becoming dependent on the teacher rather than using his own resources and knowledge to solve problems.

Teacher-Scheduled Small-Group Conferences

The group conference permits the teacher to support several children with similar needs. For instance, if three or four children are experiencing difficulty with revising their stories, the teacher might conduct a group conference that focuses on this area of need. As with the individual conference, the group meeting is no longer than five minutes.

Peer Conferences

The children are taught how to conduct peer conferences with each other. They begin the conference by reading their pieces to each other. Then they ask specific questions to clarify the meaning or extend the message. A peer conference should be brief and helpful, allowing the writer to return to her piece and resume writing. The peer's role is to listen to the author and provide constructive feedback at the meaning level. Here are four specific questions that peers should keep in mind as they listen to the writer:

> What is the writing piece about?
> Is any part of the piece confusing?
> What do I need to know more about to clarify meaning?
> What do I like about this piece?

Teacher Drop-in Conferences

In addition to daily scheduled conferences, the teacher conducts several drop-in conferences. These might occur at the beginning or end of the conferencing block. Drop-in conferences are important because they allow the teacher to observe the students' writing habits and provide brief comments on their work (Figure 5.2).

A Closer Look at Conferences

The conference consists of three major parts: the preconference, the heart of the conference, and the postconference. The preconference sets the tone for the entire session. Here, the teacher must ensure that the child takes an active role in directing her own learning. During the heart of the conference, the teacher's role is that of mediator. For example, she coaches the student to work out problems by giving hints and reminders. In the final phase of the conference, the teacher concludes the session with comments such as, "Now what do you need to do after I'm gone?" Here, the child is guided to articulate her plan for independently working on her writing. The entire conference consists of language scaffolds that are adjusted to accommodate the student's competence on various aspects of the writing process. The following are examples of teacher prompts for writing conferences:

> Show me where you are in your writing.
> What can I do to help you?
> What is your best part?
> Why do you like this part?
> Where are you having difficulty?
> What can you do to help yourself?
> Read this aloud and listen to how it sounds.
> I don't understand this part. Can you explain it to me?
> Can you think of another way to say this?
> I really like this part. Tell me more about it.

Figure 5.2 Dana conducts drop-in conferences with students.

A Teacher-Scheduled Conference on Editing

Let's look at a typical teacher-scheduled conference in a first-grade classroom. In this example, Annita Bogard, a first-grade literacy coach, meets with Tyler for an editing session. The student has written an informational report about guinea pigs and is ready to prepare the piece for publication. Tyler comes to the conference with his writing notebook, editing checklist, and written report (Figure 5.3). Annita looks at his work and begins the pre-conference, "Show me where you are in your writing." Tyler pulls over his editing checklist and says, "I want to publish my report, but there are some words I haven't corrected yet." Annita comments, "Yes, I see that you have circled most of your words and you've looked them up in your dictionary. That's good checking. But I see three circled words that you haven't corrected yet. Which one would you like my help with?" With this comment, Annita places Tyler in charge of self-directing his own learning. He leans forward and points to the word *miles*, which he has misspelled as *miyol*. Now the meat of the conference begins; in this case, to help Tyler make final spelling corrections. Annita remarks, "Why don't you try to spell it by yourself, and I'll help you if you need me." Then she pulls over a trial sheet and comments, "Well, I see that you have gotten the

Figure 5.3 Tyler's edited draft of an informational report (first grade).

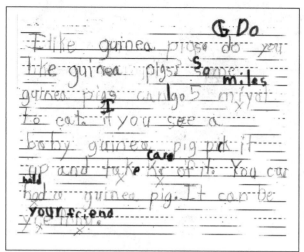

m. I believe if you say the word slowly, you can get the other letters." Tyler says the word slowly and records the letters, except for the final *e*. Annita remarks, "You're almost correct. What letter would you expect to see at the end of the word to make it look right?" "*E!*" Tyler exclaims. "Yes," says Annita. "Now you can write it in your story. Do you think you can correct one of the other words?" After Tyler corrects another word, Annita remarks, "Now, there is still one more word that you've misspelled. Would you like for me to correct it?" She asks this question because she wants the student to monitor his appeals for help, including when and when not to seek assistance. In the final moments of the conference, Annita redirects Tyler's attention to the editing checklist. "What have you already checked?" Tyler glances at the checklist. "Oops, I forgot to check the punctuation." "Do you want to do this now?" she asks. "Yes," he comments, "I'd really like to publish my writing." So, with their heads together, Annita and Tyler quickly locate three places where punctuation should be included. The final phase of the conference is the postconference. This occurs at the point when the teacher prepares to leave the student to work alone. "Now," says Annita, "what do you need to do after I'm gone?" Tyler remarks, "I need to rewrite my report." As Annita walks away, Tyler is already absorbed in preparing his piece for publication.

A Small-Group Conference on Word Choices

In a diverse classroom, the observant teacher will look for opportunities to meet with students of similar needs in a small-group setting. This will allow her to provide focused instruction on a particular skill, strategy, or craft. The social context of the group will also promote collaboration and problem-solving opportunities among peers. Here, Teresa notes that three first-graders are ready to learn about word choices. She bases this on her observations of their revising strategies, for the students are writing multiple drafts and using proofreading techniques to add and delete words and ideas. She believes the students would benefit from a conference on substituting better choices for words. She realizes this is a complex strategy that is grounded in a student's vocabulary knowledge, but the Word Choices form should be a helpful resource in applying this strategy. Thus, Teresa uses a short piece of her own writing and models the process. She shows them how to circle the word and replace this word with another word. She explains how writers do this when they think of a better way to say something. Then she invites the group to read their pieces silently and find one or two words that they might want to change. The students circle the word, record a substitute word on their Word Choices form, and share their choices with the group. As the conference comes to an end, Teresa suggests the students read through their entire piece and apply this strategy to other words.

During independent work, we can see how Devika has used this strategy to consider word choices in her story "My Birthday Party" (Figure 5.4a). She uses a yellow highlighter to mark four words, *incredibly*, *little*, *sloped*, and *forgot*. She records three of these words on her Word Choices form (Figure 5.4b) and reflects on other words that might be better choices. Then she writes her final choice in the last column. If she chooses to keep an original word in

Figure 5.4b Devika's Word Choices form.

My word	Other words	Final choice
incredibly	Unbelievably	incredibly
little	slightly	slightly
Sloped	slanted	slanted

Figure 5.4a Devika's draft showing her word choices work (first grade).

her story, she simply places a check mark above this word in her text, as she did with the word *forgot*.

A Student-Scheduled Conference on Publishing

A student might request a conference when he needs immediate help; for instance, Phillip, a first-grader, is ready to prepare his writing for publication. Earlier in the week, Carla had presented a mini-lesson on publication, but at the time Phillip was not ready for this. Carla realizes this is a new skill for Phillip; therefore, she is pleased that he has requested a conference. He brings his writing notebook and pulls out his Student-Scheduled Conferences form, a publishing checklist, and the edited version of his story (Figure 5.5). Carla notes that he has already edited his piece for capitalization, spelling, and punctuation. Also, he has begun to think about text organization; for example, he has used his red pen to separate the first sentence from the rest of the piece. As the conference begins, Carla prompts Phillip to read his story and think about sentences that he would like to place on each page. They discuss the importance of grouping ideas; and Carla scaffolds him as he clusters sentences together for five pages of text. They continue to revisit the steps on the publishing checklist: as each step is completed, Phillip places a check mark next to the step. At the end of the conference, Carla asks, "What do you need to do now?" Phillip responds, "I need to draw my pictures and write the author's page."

A Drop-in Conference with Kindergarten Students

In this final example, let's look at a kindergarten drop-in conference. Prior to independent writing, Cathy Worley, the teacher, had engaged the students in an interactive writing lesson. At this point, the students are learning how to balance the composing and transcribing processes. They can hold a simple sentence in their head, and they have acquired some early conventions of print (spacing, return sweep, concept of word and letter). They've learned to use their ABC chart as a beginning resource in two important ways: forming letters and matching letters to sounds. They have accumulated a list of approximately ten high-frequency words that they can write with accuracy (most of the time). In a drop-in conference, Cathy mingles among the students to provide support in needed areas. It is important to note that a conference always begins with the teacher's response to the meaning of the story. Here is a snippet of Cathy's interaction with Maddie about her story (Figure 5.6).

Teacher: Read me your story.
Maddie: I like ladybugs because they bring you luck.
Teacher: That's a great story. I'm so glad you told me ladybugs bring luck. I didn't know that, and your story taught me something new!

Cathy and Maddie discuss the story for a few moments, then Cathy guides Maddie to attend to her print knowledge. First, she writes the accurate spellings under Maddie's words; then she praises Maddie for her problem-solving work.

Teacher: Maddie, you've done some good work on writing your story. Look at all the sounds that you heard!

Then, Cathy uses explicit language and actions to direct Maddie's attention to the correct letter-sound matches. As she prepares to leave the

Figure 5.5 Phillip's edited draft being readied for publication (first grade).

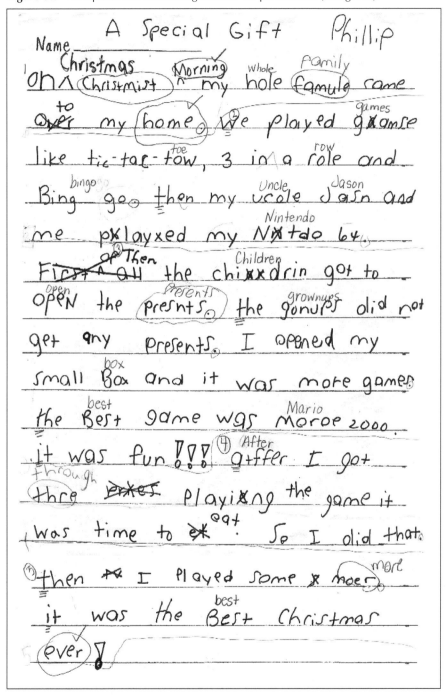

conference, she offers explicit praise. "I like the way you used your ABC chart to help with writing your letters; and you said your words slowly to hear the sounds in the words. You know a lot of ways to help yourself, don't you?" Maddie beams with pleasure and

Figure 5.6 Maddie's story on ladybugs (kindergarten).

responds, "I do!" As Cathy walks away, Maddie turns to a clean page in her journal and begins writing a new story.

Closing Thoughts

In this chapter, we have emphasized the importance of the writing conference during writers' workshop. It is here that the teacher can scaffold the writer with personalized and tailored support. Talking about writing provides young writers with tools for articulating and reflecting on their own work. Throughout this book, we have presented details for imple-

menting writers' workshop in the primary grades. We have discussed the link between assessment and teaching, and we have advocated for explicit teaching that is grounded in students' knowledge. During the act of writing, children acquire understanding of the writing process, and they refine the writing craft through good models and expert guidance. One thing we know for sure is that children become better writers through successful experiences with writing. Teachers scaffold young writers by providing them with meaningful and relevant opportunities to learn how to write.

Appendixes

Appendix A

First-Grade Writing Proficiency Benchmark/Narrative Writing

Standard I—Process and Habits   **38 points**

First Draft
- ✓ Records ideas with fluency (2 points)   _____
- ✓ Rereads what has been written (2 points)   _____

Revising
- ✓ Adds/deletes words (4 points)   _____
  - • Rearranges words, sentences, or phrases (2 points)   _____
  - • Substitutes richer vocabulary choices (2 points)   _____
- ✓ Uses writing checklist (4 points)   _____

Editing
- ✓ Notices some errors in spelling by circling words (4 points)   _____
  - • Corrects many misspelled words (2 points)   _____
  - • Corrects some punctuation and capitalization (2 points)   _____
- ✓ Uses resources to check (e.g., dictionary, checklists) (4 points)   _____
  - • Uses a thesaurus (2 points)   _____

Final Draft
- ✓ Incorporates revisions into final copy (4 points)   _____
- ✓ Increases accuracy of the final draft (spelling, punctuation)
  (4 points)   _____

                                                              Total   _____

Standard I
_____ Below the Standard (19 or less)
_____ Approaching the Standard (20–27)
_____ Meeting the Standard (28)
_____ Exceeding the Standard (above 28)

Standard II—Audience and Purposes/Author's Craft   **59 points**

Introduces the Topic
- ✓ Opening sentence states focus of writing (10 points)   _____
  - • Grabs the attention of the reader (2 points)   _____

Develops the Topic
- ✓ Uses logical order (beginning, middle, end) (6 points)   _____
- ✓ Sustains the idea throughout the piece (6 points)   _____
  - • Uses dialogue (3 points)   _____
  - • Uses individual voice (3 points)   _____
  - • Uses reaction phrases (3 points)   _____
- ✓ Uses transitional and time cue words to support flow (5 points)   _____
- ✓ Uses some strong vocabulary and word choice [more than
  1 word] (e.g., *shouted* for *said, huge* for *big*) (5 points)   _____
  - • Uses several interesting words to express ideas (2 points)   _____
  - • Begins to use descriptive and figurative language (2 points)   _____

Concludes the Topic
- ✓ Provides sense of closure (e.g., "It was fun." "This ends my story."
  "The end.") (10 points)   _____
  - • Ties story together with creative or imaginative ending (2 points)   _____
                                                              Total   _____

Standard II
_____ Below the Standard (35 or less)
_____ Approaching the Standard (36–41)
_____ Meeting the Standard (42)
_____ Exceeding the Standard (above 42)

Scaffolding Young Writers: A Writers' Workshop Approach by Linda J. Dorn and Carla Soffos. Copyright © 2001. Stenhouse Publishers

Appendix A

Standard III—Language Use and Conventions 37 points

Style and Syntax
- ✓ Uses a variety of sentence structures and lengths (3 points) _____
  - Shows evidence of book language or structures from other texts (2 points) _____

Spelling
- ✓ Writes most high-frequency words correctly (5 points) _____
  - Writes all high-frequency words correctly (2 points) _____
- ✓ Uses phonetic spelling (5 points) _____
  - Uses transitional and/or conventional spelling (2 points) _____

Punctuation and Conventions
- ✓ Writes complete sentences majority of the time (3 points) _____
  - Writes complete sentences all of the time (3 points) _____
  - Uses subject/verb agreement most of the time (2 points) _____
- ✓ Demonstrates some accurate use of beginning capitalization (4 points) _____
  - Demonstrates mostly accurate use of beginning capitalization (2 points) _____
- ✓ Demonstrates some accurate use of closing punctuation (periods and question marks) (2 points) _____
  - Demonstrates mostly accurate use of closing punctuation (periods and question marks) (2 points) _____

Total _____

Standard III
_____ Below the Standard (16 or less)
_____ Approaching the Standard (17–22)
_____ Meeting the Standard (22)
_____ Exceeding the Standard (above 22)

Appendix A

Second-Grade Writing Proficiency Benchmark/Narrative Writing

Standard I—Process and Habits   **48 points**

Standard I

_____ Below the Standard (29 or less)

_____ Approaching the Standard (30–35)

_____ Meeting the Standard (36)

_____ Exceeding the Standard (above 36)

First Draft
✓ Uses prewriting strategies to plan and organize ideas (2 points)   _____

Revising
✓ Adds/deletes words or ideas (6 points)   _____
   • Rearranges words, sentences, or phrases (4 points)   _____
✓ Substitutes richer vocabulary (3 points)   _____
✓ Uses writing checklist (3 points)   _____

Editing
✓ Notices many errors in spelling by circling words (3 points)   _____
✓ Attempts to correct most misspelled words (3 points)   _____
   • Attempts to correct all misspelled words (2 points)   _____
✓ Corrects most punctuation and capitalization (6 points)   _____
   • Corrects all punctuation and capitalization (2 points)   _____
✓ Uses resources to check (e.g., dictionary, checklists) (4 points)   _____
   • Uses a thesaurus (2 points)   _____

Final Draft
✓ Incorporates revisions into final copy (4 points)   _____
✓ Increases accuracy of the final draft (spelling, punctuation) (4 points)   _____

                                                          Total   _____

Standard II—Audience and Purposes/Author's Craft   **54 points**

Standard II

_____ Below the Standard (32 or less)

_____ Approaching the Standard (32–41)

_____ Meeting the Standard (42)

_____ Exceeding the Standard (above 42)

Introduces the Topic
✓ Opening sentence(s) states focus of writing (6 points)   _____
   • Creates a good lead that grabs the reader's attention (4 points)   _____

Develops the Topic
✓ Uses logical order (beginning, middle, end) (6 points)   _____
✓ Sustains the idea throughout the piece (6 points)   _____
✓ Uses individual voice (4 points)   _____
   • Uses dialogue effectively (2 points)   _____
✓ Uses transitional words for time flow (3 points)   _____
   • Uses transitional phrases for time flow (2 points)   _____
✓ Uses strong nouns and muscular verbs (4 points)   _____
✓ Uses descriptive words to create mind pictures (4 points)   _____
   • Uses figurative language, similes, or metaphors (2 points)   _____
✓ Writes to the prompt (3 points)   _____

Concludes the Topic
✓ Provides sense of closure (e.g., "It was fun." "This ends my story." "The end.") (6 points)   _____
   • Ties story together with appropriate and interesting sentence or section (2 points)   _____

                                                          Total   _____

Appendix A

Standard III—Language Use and Conventions 39 points

Style and Syntax
- ✓ Uses a variety of sentence structures and lengths (4 points) _____
- ✓ Shows evidence of book language, specialized vocabulary, or structures from other texts (4 points) _____
- ✓ Writes correct sentences the majority of the time (2 points) _____
  - • Writes correct sentences all the time (free of run-ons/ fragments) (2 points) _____

Spelling
- ✓ Accurate spelling of most high-frequency words (2 points) _____
  - • Accurate spelling of all high-frequency words (2 points) _____
- ✓ Uses transitional and/or conventional spelling (4 points) _____

Punctuation and Conventions
- ✓ Uses pronouns correctly (3 points) _____
- ✓ Uses subject/verb agreement (2 points) _____
- ✓ Uses end punctuation correctly most of the time (3 points) _____
  - • Uses end punctuation correctly all the time (2 points) _____
  - • Uses additional forms of punctuation correctly (3 points) _____
  - • Indents paragraphs (2 points) _____
- ✓ Uses correct capitalization including beginning of sentences and proper nouns most of the time (2 points) _____
  - • Uses correct capitalization including beginning of sentences and proper nouns all the time (2 points) _____

Total _____

Standard III
_____ Below the Standard (19 or less)
_____ Approaching the Standard (20–25)
_____ Meeting the Standard (26)
_____ Exceeding the Standard (above 26)

Appendix A

Third-Grade Writing Proficiency Benchmark/Narrative Writing

Standard I—Process and Habits   **54 points**

First Draft

✓ Uses prewriting strategies to plan and organize ideas (2 points) _____

Revising

✓ Adds/deletes words or ideas (6 points)   _____
✓ Rearranges words, sentences, or phrases (4 points)   _____
✓ Substitutes richer vocabulary (4 points)   _____
✓ Uses writing checklist (2 points)   _____

Editing

✓ Notices most errors in spelling by circling words (4 points)   _____
✓ Attempts to correct most misspelled words (4 points)   _____
  • Attempts to correct all misspelled words (2 points)   _____
✓ Corrects all punctuation and capitalization (6 points)   _____
✓ Uses resources to check (e.g., dictionary, checklists) (6 points) _____
  • Uses a thesaurus (2 points)   _____

Final Draft

✓ Incorporates revisions into final copy (6 points)   _____
✓ Increases accuracy of the final draft (spelling, punctuation)
  (6 points)   _____

                                               Total   _____

Standard I
_____ Below the Standard (31 or less)
_____ Approaching the Standard (32–49)
_____ Meeting the Standard (50)
_____ Exceeding the Standard (above 50)

Standard II—Audience and Purposes/Author's Craft   **56 points**

Introduces the Topic

✓ Creates a good lead that grabs the reader's attention (8 points) _____

Develops the Topic

✓ Uses logical order (beginning, middle, end) (6 points)   _____
✓ Sustains the idea throughout the piece (6 points)   _____
✓ Uses individual voice (4 points)   _____
✓ Uses dialogue effectively (4 points)   _____
✓ Uses transitional words/phrases for time flow (5 points)   _____
✓ Uses strong nouns and muscular verbs (4 points)   _____
✓ Uses descriptive words to create mind pictures (4 points)   _____
✓ Uses figurative language, similes, or metaphors (4 points)   _____
✓ Writes to the prompt (3 points)   _____

Concludes the Topic

✓ Ties story together with appropriate and interesting sentence
  or section (8 points)   _____

                                               Total   _____

Standard II
_____ Below the Standard (32 or less)
_____ Approaching the Standard (32–47)
_____ Meeting the Standard (48)
_____ Exceeding the Standard (above 48)

Scaffolding Young Writers: A Writers' Workshop Approach by Linda J. Dorn and Carla Soffos. Copyright © 2001. Stenhouse Publishers

Appendix A

Standard III—Language Use and Conventions   **39 points**

Style and Syntax
- ✓ Uses a variety of sentence structures and lengths (4 points) _____
- ✓ Shows evidence of book language, specialized vocabulary,
  or structures from other texts (4 points) _____
- ✓ Writes correct sentences all the time (free of run-ons/
  fragments (4 points) _____

Spelling
- ✓ Accurate spelling of all high-frequency words (4 points) _____
- ✓ Uses transitional and/or conventional spelling (4 points) _____

Punctuation and Conventions
- ✓ Uses pronouns correctly (3 points) _____
- ✓ Uses subject/verb agreement (3 points) _____
- ✓ Uses end punctuation correctly all the time (4 points) _____
  - • Uses additional forms of punctuation correctly (3 points) _____
  - • Indents paragraphs (2 points) _____
- ✓ Uses correct capitalization including beginning of sentences
  and proper nouns all the time (4 points) _____

                                                       Total _____

Standard III
- _____ Below the Standard (19 or less)
- _____ Approaching the Standard (20–33)
- _____ Meeting the Standard (34)
- _____ Exceeding the Standard (above 34)

Appendix B

Writing Checklist

Name _____   **Date** _____

Teacher _____   **Grade** _____

Writing Process and Craft	+ -	Comments
Understands steps of writing process		
Generates topics and writing ideas		
Adds details to support topic ideas		
Arranges events in sequential order		
Shows character development		
Uses dialogue		
Writes for different purposes and audiences		
Revises texts for word choice and meaning		
Edits texts for spelling and punctuation		
Uses checklists and rubrics to self-evaluate		
Uses the dictionary to check spelling		
Publishes and shares work		

Writing Language and Mechanics		
Uses knowledge of genre structure		
Uses figurative language, similes, and metaphors		
Uses a variety of sentence structures		
Uses paragraph structure		
Uses ending punctuation correctly		
Uses quotation marks and commas		
Uses capital letters appropriately		
Aware of subject/verb agreement (edits for this in writers' workshop)		
Aware of correct pronoun usage (edits for this in writers' workshop)		
Forms complete sentences		

Writing Texts Completed (Circle, date, attach with genre checklist)

Autobiography _____   Directions, instructions _____

Biography _____   Recipe _____

Report _____   Letter, note _____

Tall Tale, Folk Tale _____   Story retelling _____

Fairy Tale _____   Story innovation _____

Mystery _____   Poetry _____

Scaffolding Young Writers: A Writers' Workshop Approach by Linda J. Dorn and Carla Soffos. Copyright © 2001. Stenhouse Publishers

Appendix B

Checklist for Tall Tales

1. What is the title of the tall tale?

2. Describe the setting. In what country or region does it take place?

3. Who is the hero/heroine?

4. Describe the qualities of hero/heroine.

5. Who are the other characters in the story?

6. Describe the qualities of the other characters.

7. What was the hardship to overcome in the story?

8. How was the hardship solved?

9. What exaggerations are used in the tall tale?

Appendix C

Writing Process

Think   Think about a topic for writing.

Plan   Plan your topic.

Write   Write your text.

Revise   Add to your text and X out what you don't want.

Move around your text if needed.

Use the best words to describe your idea.

Edit   Circle the words that do not look right.

Look up the circled words in the dictionary or other resources.

Check for punctuation and capitalization.

Publish   Rewrite final draft to be shared with an audience.

Appendix D

Student-Scheduled Conferences

Story Title	Plan	Draft	Revise	Edit	? Publishing ?	
					yes	no
					yes	no
					yes	no
					yes	no
					yes	no
					yes	no
					yes	no
					yes	no
					yes	no
					yes	no
					yes	no
					yes	no
					yes	no

Appendix D

Topic List

_____   _____

_____   _____

_____   _____

_____   _____

_____   _____

_____   _____

_____   _____

_____   _____

Appendix D

Books That Spark an Idea

Book Title _____

Book Title _____

Book Title _____

Book Title _____

Book Title _____

Book Title _____

Appendix D

Action Words

_____   _____

_____   _____

_____   _____

_____   _____

_____   _____

_____   _____

_____   _____

_____   _____

_____   _____

_____   _____

_____   _____

_____   _____

Appendix D

Describing Words

_____   _____

_____   _____

_____   _____

_____   _____

_____   _____

_____   _____

_____   _____

_____   _____

_____   _____

_____   _____

_____   _____

_____   _____

_____   _____

Appendix D

Writing Checklist

1. Read your story out loud to make sure it makes sense. _____

2. Add to your story or X out what you don't want. _____

3. Circle words that do not look right. _____

4. Use trial page to check spellings. _____

5. Look up the circled words. _____

6. Read your story out loud. Listen for where your voice stops. Add punctuation. _____

7. Check for capitalization at the beginning of your sentences. _____

Scaffolding Young Writers: A Writers' Workshop Approach by Linda J. Dorn and Carla Soffos. Copyright © 2001. Stenhouse Publishers

Appendix D

Publishing a Book

Read your story and decide how to organize the sentences into a book.

Use a red pen to separate your story into pages. _____

How many pages will you need? Gather the number of pages for your book. _____

Rewrite the story in your neatest writing. _____

Draw the pictures on each page to illustrate your story. _____

Write the title and author on the cover page. _____

Write an author's page at the end of your book. _____

Staple or bind your book. _____

Share your book. _____

Appendix D

My Trial Page

First Try	Second Try	Correct

Appendix D

Word Choices

My Word	Other Words	Final Choice

Appendix E

Text Guide for Writing Informational Texts

1. Choose your topic.

_____

_____

_____

_____

2. Use up-to-date and accurate resources to learn about your topic.

_____

_____

_____

_____

3. Use notes or diagrams to organize your information.

_____

_____

_____

_____

4. Use a good opening sentence to introduce your topic.

_____

_____

_____

_____

Appendix E

Checklist for Informational Texts

1. Did you use up-to-date and accurate resources to learn about your topic? _____

2. Did you use notes or diagrams to organize your information? _____

3. Did you use a good opening sentence to introduce your topic? _____

4. Did you organize your information in an orderly format? _____

5. Did you include accurate facts? _____

6. Did you add details to explain your topic in clear language? _____

7. Did you use a closing statement? _____

Appendix F

Checklist for Mystery

1. Did you include a main character? _____

2. Did you describe the main character? _____

3. Did you include other characters? _____

4. Did you describe the setting? _____

5. Did you describe the mystery to be solved? _____

6. Did you sprinkle clues throughout to help solve the mystery? _____

7. Did you explain how the mystery was solved? _____

Appendix G

Written Retelling

1. Write a good lead that grabs the attention of the reader. _____

2. Write what happened first. _____

3. Write what happened next. _____

4. Write what happened last. _____

5. Include interesting details to describe the events. _____

6. Use an appropriate ending. _____

7. React to the story in a personal way. _____

Appendix H

Teacher-Scheduled Conferences

Student	Plan	Draft	Revise	Edit	Final	Teacher Notes

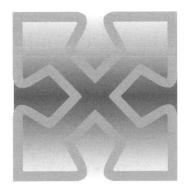

References

Briton, J. 1970. *Language and Learning.* Harmondsworth, UK: Penguin Books.

Calkins, L. 1986. *The Art of Teaching Writing.* Portsmouth, NH: Heinemann.

Carle, E. 1969. *The Very Hungry Caterpillar.* New York: Philomel Books.

Clay, M. 2001. *Change Over Time in Children's Literacy Development.* Portsmouth, NH: Heinemann.

Clemens, A. 1997. *Big Al.* Old Tappan, NJ: Simon and Schuster.

Dorn, L. 1999. *Learning About Writing.* One of the videotapes in *Organizing for Literacy.* Portland, ME: Stenhouse.

Dorn, L., C. French, and T. Jones. 1998. *Apprenticeship in Literacy: Transitions Across Reading and Writing.* Portland, ME: Stenhouse.

Dorn, L., and C. Soffos. 2001a. *Shaping Literate Minds: Developing Self-Regulated Learners.* Portland, ME: Stenhouse.

———. 2001b. *Writers Inservice Videotape.* San Diego: Teaching Resource Center.

Fletcher, R., and J. Portalupi. 1998. *Craft Lessons: Teaching Writing K–8.* Portland, ME: Stenhouse.

Graves, D. 1994. *A Fresh Look at Writing.* Portsmouth, NH: Heinemann.

Harris, K., and S. Graham. 1999. *Making the Writing Process Work: Strategies for Composition and Self-Regulation.* Cambridge, MA: Brookline Books.

Healy, J. 1994. *Your Child's Growing Mind.* New York: Doubleday

New Standards Primary Committee. 1999. *Reading and Writing Grade by Grade: Primary Literacy Standards for Kindergarten Through Third Grade.* Washington, DC: National Center on Education and the Economy and the University of Pittsburgh.

Oxenbury, H., illus. 1968. *The Great Big Enormous Turnip,* by A. Tolstoi. New York: Watts.

Pfister, M. 1992. *The Rainbow Fish.* Trans. J. A. James. New York: North-South Books.

Showers, P. 1991. *The Listening Walk.* New York: HarperCollins.

Silverstein, S. 1964. *The Giving Tree.* New York: Harper and Row.

Smith, F. 1994. *Writing and the Writer.* Hillsdale, NJ: Lawrence Erlbaum.

Vygotsky, L. 1978. *Mind in Society: The Development of Higher Psychological Processes,* ed. M. Cole, V. John-Steiner, S. Scribner, and E. Souberman. Cambridge, MA: Harvard University Press.

Index

Shaping Literate Minds

Developing Self-Regulated Learners

Linda J. Dorn and Carla Soffos

How can teachers create a literacy curriculum that builds processing links between reading, writing, and spelling knowledge? In *Shaping Literate Minds*, Linda Dorn and Carla Soffos illustrate how processing theory can be applied to the everyday practices of classroom teaching.

If instruction emphasizes the interrelationships of these three language areas, students learn how to transfer knowledge, skills, and strategies across literacy events. This is complex theory, but the authors provide clear and practical examples to support teachers as they incorporate these ideas into their classroom practices.

Grounded in authentic experiences from primary classrooms, this book provides:

- explanations of processing behaviors among reading, writing, and spelling knowledge;
- observational tools that support teachers in noticing changes over time in specific literacy behaviors;
- guidance on creating conditions for developing self-regulated learners;
- authentic reading and writing samples and teacher/student interactions;
- figures and pictures that clearly describe how teachers can use assessment to inform and guide instruction, with links to national standards;
- details for establishing a school-based literacy model that includes team meetings, assessment walls, high standards, and a curriculum for literacy;
- appendixes with reproducible assessment checklists, report cards, task cards for literacy corners, and guided reading observation forms for team meetings.

With a national emphasis on accountability, high standards, and literacy achievement, *Shaping Literate Minds* will help teachers and administrators implement a high-quality literacy curriculum that links to national and state goals

Organizing for Literacy

Four Inservice Videotapes

Linda J. Dorn

Organizing for Literacy is a professional development series for implementing a balanced early literacy program that uses apprenticeship theory. When used in conjunction with the book *Apprenticeship in Literacy,* the series presents a complete early literacy resource, with the option of using individual videos to focus on a specific area of need.

The tapes illustrate the reciprocal nature of teaching and learning across a range of reading and writing events. Each tape is designed to allow you to view it in its entirety or to focus on specific literacy components. The accompanying viewing guide is structured to promote the analysis of teaching and learning interactions during these components. Also, the tapes can be cross-referenced for evidence of how the same children are applying their knowledge, skills, and strategies across a range of reading, writing, and word-building activities. Since this is an important principle of apprenticeship literacy, a chart for cross-referencing teaching segments across the four tapes is included at the end of the viewing guide.

**Contact your local distributor or call
800-988-9812 • www.stenhouse.com**

Apprenticeship in Literacy

Transitions Across Reading and Writing

Linda J. Dorn, Cathy French, and Tammy Jones

This easy-to-read text will guide K–3 teachers as they develop a reading and writing program for all their students. An apprenticeship approach to literacy emphasizes the role of the teacher in providing demonstrations, engaging children, monitoring their understanding, providing timely support and, ultimately, withdrawing that support as the child gains independence.

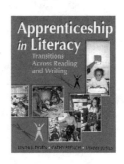

Drawing on authentic classroom examples—student writing samples, class schedules, photographs, and rich transcriptions of teaching and learning interactions—the authors illustrate instruction that is aimed at children's learning zones. As children become more competent readers and writers, the instructional interactions are adjusted to accommodate their higher-level learning.

Here is a wealth of in-depth information, specific strategies, and organizational formats in many literacy areas. The authors cover such practical matters as establishing routines and organizing the classroom environment, including rotation schedules for meeting with small groups of children, lists of materials for establishing literacy corners, and literacy corner activities designed to provide children with opportunities for independent practice.